Own Your AWKWARD THOUGHTS

master the art of REFRAMING
the way you think

ANDY VARGO

Own Your Awkward Thoughts

Text copyright © 2022 by Andy Vargo

All Rights Reserved

ISBN 979-8-9897351-0-5

Awkward Career Publications

awkwardcareer.com

All rights reserved. No part of this publication may be reproduced, distributed, or transmitted in any form or by any means, including photocopying, recording, or other electronic or mechanical methods, without the prior written permission of the publisher, except in the case of brief quotations embodied in critical reviews and certain other noncommercial uses permitted by copyright law.

Sometimes you just need to change the way you are looking at life.

I say it all the time to clients and friends alike, *If you want to change the way you live, you have to change the way you think.*

But it isn't that easy. Thinking happens behind the scenes day and night whether you are conscious of your thoughts or not.

Even worse is that you have spent a lifetime thinking the same way. How can you compete with a force like that?

Practice. Awareness.

Practicing awareness.

It comes down to practice. If you want to get good at anything, you have to put in the hours.

Just like any talent or skill you want to master, you can practice how you think. And so doing, you can start living the life you want to live.

The upcoming pages are filled with reflections to help you do just that, change the way you think.

These are the raw thoughts that run through my mind in any given moment. They are captured as I sit in the moment and gain my own mental awareness.

Picture yourself at a cafe, in a park or even on the side of the road, only to look over to see a stranger frantically writing down words before they are lost forever.

That stranger is me, in the moment, capturing the raw feelings as I work through the moment to transform an idea, an emotion, or an event, into the way of thinking I want for the life I choose.

Those thoughts fill these pages. They are the work I have done, and continually do, to change the way I think. To reframe the moments in life that don't always feel so great.

And it works!

Now they are my gift for you in hopes that you can do the same for yourself.

Read them. Enjoy them. But most of all, reflect on the way they might relate to where you are right now in life. Where you have been, and where you want to be.

Then spend some time on the reflections in order to help take your mind and your life in the direction you want to go.

Because sometimes you feel great.

Sometimes you feel scared.

Sometimes you think the world will never change.

And sometimes you just need to change the way you think.

Opening Thoughts

Before we step into the daily reflections, I'd like to arm you with a few questions to ask yourself in order to take your thinking in a different direction.

The reflections in this book are from my own moments of self-discovery. The opening thought is how I felt at the start of an experience.

By the end of the reflection, I have paused my mind, asked myself one or more of the questions I am going to share with you now, then turned my thinking into the alternative thoughts I share with you by the end.

Reframing your thoughts is a critical skill in living the life you want to have. Situations will continue to get dropped in your lap. Your brain will react the way it has spent years learning to respond.

The natural instinct to think a certain way is okay. Understand before you move forward that there is nothing wrong with the fact that you are inclined to think the way you have always thought.

Identifying it and learning to turn your thoughts in a different direction, is a skill you will learn and practice in the days ahead.

The questions to keep in mind and apply to any situation are in the frame on the next page. They are designed to trick your mind by looking at the situation you are currently experiencing from a different angle, a new perspective.

By answering them in this way, you are by default reframing your thoughts. You are seeing them in a way you may not instinctively view them.

Key Questions

to

Reframe Your Thoughts

∞ What is the best possible outcome of this situation?

∞ What would you tell someone else if they were going through the same thing?

∞ When have you felt like this in the past and made it through just fine?

∞ What other factors could be at play affecting how you feel right now?

∞ How can you tell this story in a different way with a better ending?

∞ What is the real issue here?

Sometimes you just know you are going to do great things.

You know it's in you. But you just don't know quite how you're going to make it happen.

You don't lack faith in yourself. It's just the process you are not sure if you trust.

It's not been a matter of if or when for a long time now.

You gave up saying if long ago and always say when.

When it happens... When I make it...

When it all comes together...

You understand why.

Why you want to. Why it's needed. Why it will be accepted by the world.

Though you're not sure about just when the when will come, you have no doubt that it will.

And when the when comes, you will be ready.

Yet you really struggle with the how.

How will you make it happen? How will you bring it all together? How do you proceed next?

Not knowing the how consumes you. It overwhelms your thoughts.

Worst of all, it undermines your faith in the when.
Don't let it my friend.

The when will come. The how will unfold along the way. I can't say what it will be. No one really can.

But it will happen.

You may even have to try a hundred hows along the way.

And suddenly one how will turn into a when.

And when it does for you, I want to be there to see it.

I want to celebrate with you then. I can't wait to say "I knew you when."

I want to be there and to say I saw you when you changed the world.

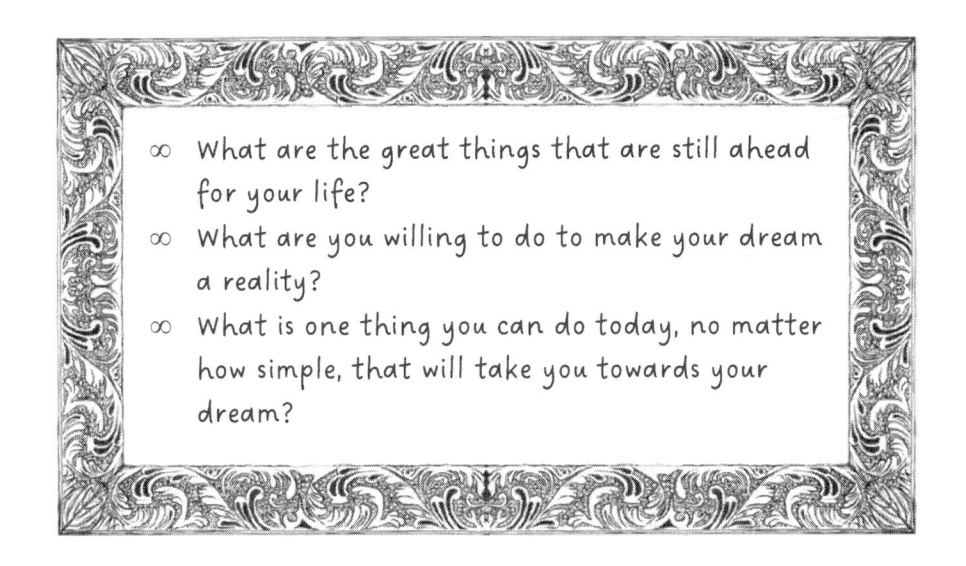

- ∞ What are the great things that are still ahead for your life?
- ∞ What are you willing to do to make your dream a reality?
- ∞ What is one thing you can do today, no matter how simple, that will take you towards your dream?

Sometimes you walk around a corner and you see a place you didn't expect to see right in front of you.

You came at it from a different angle, but there it is.

A memory is thrown in your path. You'd have to trip over it to go any further.

A lunch date. A best friend. A confession.

Tension. Laughter. Tears. Relief. Coming out to someone you love.

But now they're gone. Yet the memory remains.

They thought they knew you. But there was so much more to know. So much more to love.

You weren't sure if they'd see it that way. But why would you ever doubt their love for you?

We expect the worst from those who know us best. Ironic, isn't it? But it's true.

Maybe because it's with them that we have the most to lose. Maybe it's because we are so afraid to truly love ourselves.

Whatever the reason, its weight brings us to the bottom of an airless sea, gasping for breath. The memory stings.

Not because they turned away from you. But because they accepted you whole-heartedly, and then they were taken from you.

Teased with unconditional love for such a brief time that they really knew you. And now they are gone.

Like a firework that lights up the sky with an overwhelming brilliance, it takes your breath away. Yet only for a minute.

But would you leave the chance for brilliance behind if you knew the fire would dim? Would you rather stay forever in the darkness and not see the light, or feel the warmth? I think not.

They are gone. Yes. But their love remains. And with it, an awareness that you are worth it. That you deserve love.

The glimpse of love they shared was not meant to leave you in despair. But rather to leave you with hope. To know that love is out there. That you are loved and will be loved again.

Though death can take one love away, it readies you to accept love another day.

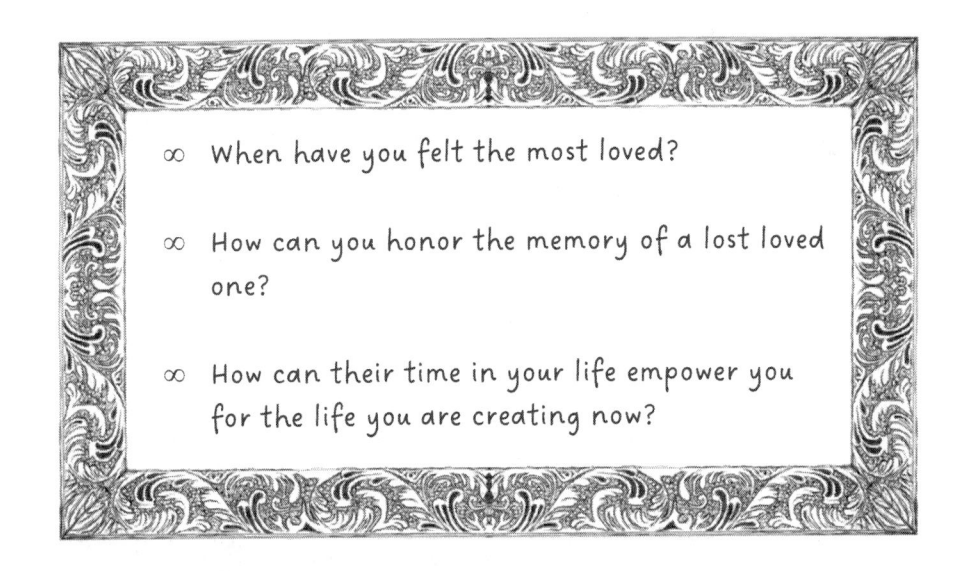

- ∞ When have you felt the most loved?
- ∞ How can you honor the memory of a lost loved one?
- ∞ How can their time in your life empower you for the life you are creating now?

Sometimes you have the most amazing thing happen yet you become the most uncomfortable you have ever felt.

You don't trust it. You fear that it is only there to hide a monster.

You believe deep down that it is luring you in, only to crush your soul when it disappears after taking your heart out to play before abandoning it in the desert.

You doubt your own worthiness to accept it into your life.
So you keep the walls up, refusing to be conned.

This feels exciting, something must be wrong. The feelings in your heart argue with the logic in your mind.

Yet the goodness still wants in. It sees the value you can't see in yourself. It begs for the door to open so it can ease in and prove its trust to you.

You relent, just barely. Just enough to be lifted a little higher by the good.

You're still afraid to go higher, but you do, knowing that it will make the drop even that much bigger when you fall.

But you don't always fall. And the good isn't always hiding bad.

You are worth having the ride and getting to that high.

So let the goodness in my friend. Don't question your worth.

Take the blessings the world brings you.
Even if it's not easy or comfortable. Especially when it's not easy or comfortable. Because those are the best of all.

It is true, whatever you seek you will find.

Look for the wind to fill your sails and take you on a great destination. Not for the wind that will blow you over.

The same wind has the power to do both. You deserve the good wind my friend.

Be ready for it. Accept it. Let it fill your sails. Know that you will never catch the good wind if your sails are lowered, and you are hiding in the cabin.

You have to keep your sails raised. But first, you have to believe in yourself. And know that you deserve to be on the most amazing journey you could ever imagine.

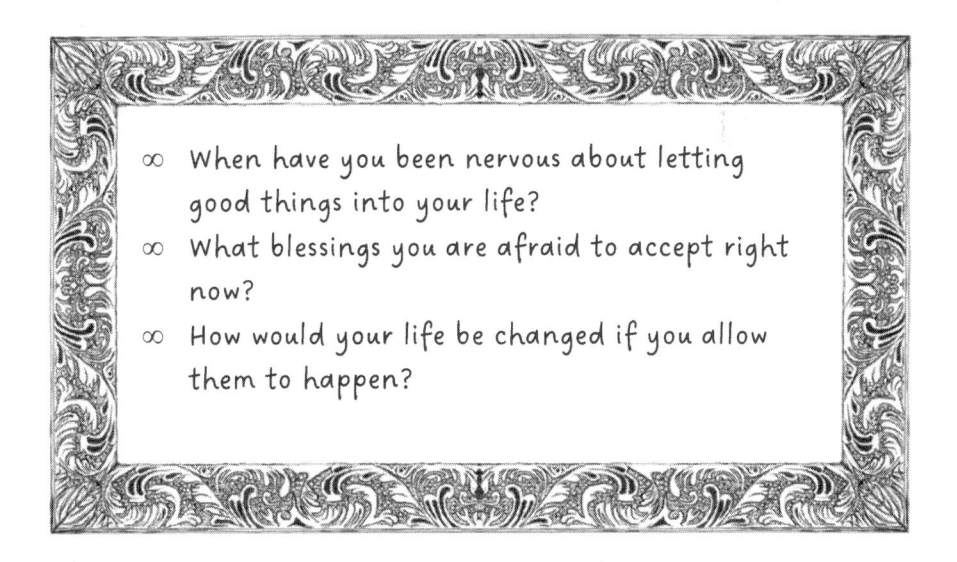

- ∞ When have you been nervous about letting good things into your life?
- ∞ What blessings you are afraid to accept right now?
- ∞ How would your life be changed if you allow them to happen?

Sometimes you wake up but you just don't feel like playing the game.

You know there are moves to be made, and worse yet, other players will keep advancing while you sit motionless.

But your heart isn't in it today.

You sit.

You observe.

You wonder when the urge to play will come back.

But for now you do nothing.

Then your mind races with the energy your body doesn't have to take action. You think about all the things which are not getting done while you take a day off from the game.

And the guilt settles in. But you just can't keep going at this pace.

You need to rest. To recharge. To refuel.

So you decide that you need to do the only thing you can: give yourself permission to take a break.

That is when the relief sets in.

When you acknowledge the role a break will play in being productive, you give it power.

You take away the guilt of not making a different move.
You begin to understand that sometimes taking a break and stepping away is the best move you can make in the game.

By making this move, you are setting yourself up for bigger and bolder moves in the future.

So remember my friend, when you don't feel like playing the game, you might need to just reframe the idea of what the right move is.

Then you can take control of the game by making a power move with a power nap like you have never had before.

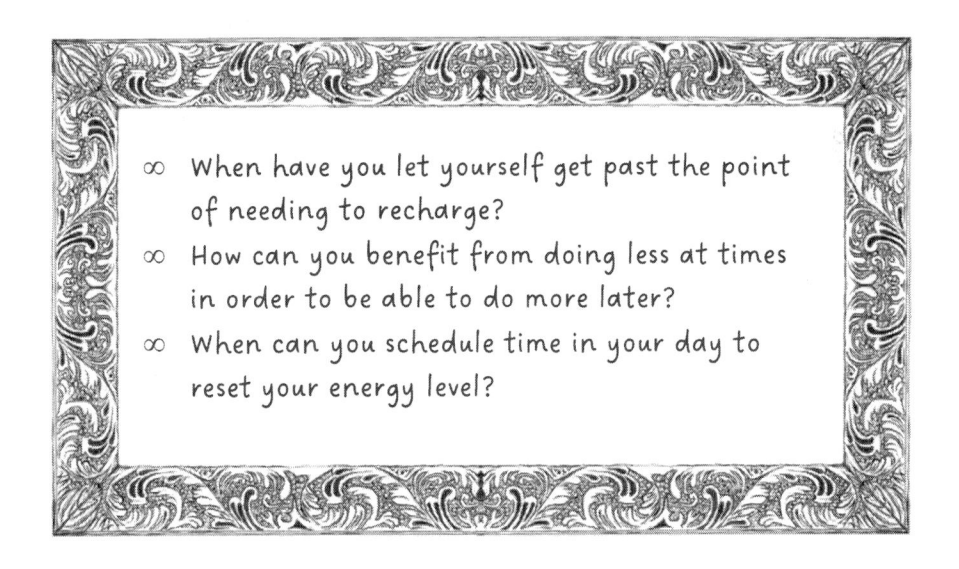

- ∞ When have you let yourself get past the point of needing to recharge?
- ∞ How can you benefit from doing less at times in order to be able to do more later?
- ∞ When can you schedule time in your day to reset your energy level?

Sometimes you encounter people who can't cope with their own emotions.

They take it out on you, whether you pick up on it right away or not.

They lash out. Giving you the cold-shoulder at the very least. Releasing their full wrath of verbal attacks or even physical at the most extreme.

You're hurt You're confused. You wonder what you've done wrong. Why do you deserve this?

You get lost in your search for answers.

But you're asking all the wrong questions.

The answers have nothing to do with you. In fact, you aren't even part of the questions. It's all on them.

You're simply the closest target. The easiest casualty in the war they are battling inside themselves.

So you feel the hurt. You absorb their pain.

You take on the problems they can't resolve in their own story.

Once you see the game they play, you find understanding.

Understanding that they have problems they can't comprehend.

Understanding that they don't hate you as much as they hate themselves.

They are only doing what they can to get by. To cope with a life they cannot understand.

It's not okay. It's not your fault. You don't deserve to be a punching bag for their unresolved issues.

But at least you can fall asleep at night knowing they are just doing the best they can. Even when it isn't right.

All you can do is the best you can. Seek to understand. And while doing so, set a hard boundary to keep them at bay.

Walk away. Run if you need to. Their issues are not for you to solve.

As you move on with your life, you can see them in their pain and be free from the guilt that you have any part in their internal struggle.

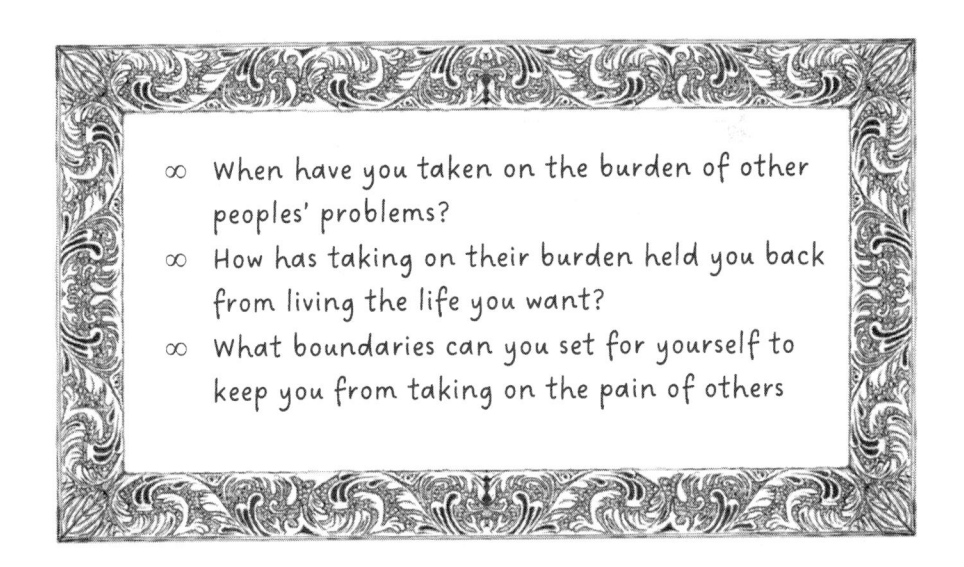

- ∞ When have you taken on the burden of other peoples' problems?
- ∞ How has taking on their burden held you back from living the life you want?
- ∞ What boundaries can you set for yourself to keep you from taking on the pain of others

Sometimes you are doing everything right.

You're following the rules, sticking to the plan, staying in your lane. When out of nowhere a force knocks you off your path.

It was not your fault. It was out of your control. You had no warning. No time to prepare.

So here you are in the after. After your world was rocked. After things changed.

Now you have choices to make.

You can choose to find fault somewhere, to blame someone. You could be right too. This might make you feel a bit better for a fleeting moment. But that doesn't change where you are now.

You can choose to curl up in a ball and mourn what was supposed to be, what could have been. But that doesn't take you out of the after either.

You can spew anger and hate towards anything or anyone around you for changing your life. But when you're done shouting you'll be even more alone and still stuck in the after.

However, those aren't the only options. They may be obvious and easy, but they are not your only choices.

You can make a new plan.

You can search for lessons from this experience.

You can clean up what needs to be cleaned up.

And you can move on.

This is life my friend. Life is about the choice you make when you shouldn't have been put in the place to make one.

Life is about learning and growing. About doing better today than you did yesterday. Because now you know more. You've experienced more.

So when you're left in the after, sit there in peace for a few moments while you reflect on what choices you will make next.

For even when something outside of your power happens, you still have the power to make the next move.

You have the power to choose.

When you decide what to do next, I hope I am there to see the amazing choices you make.

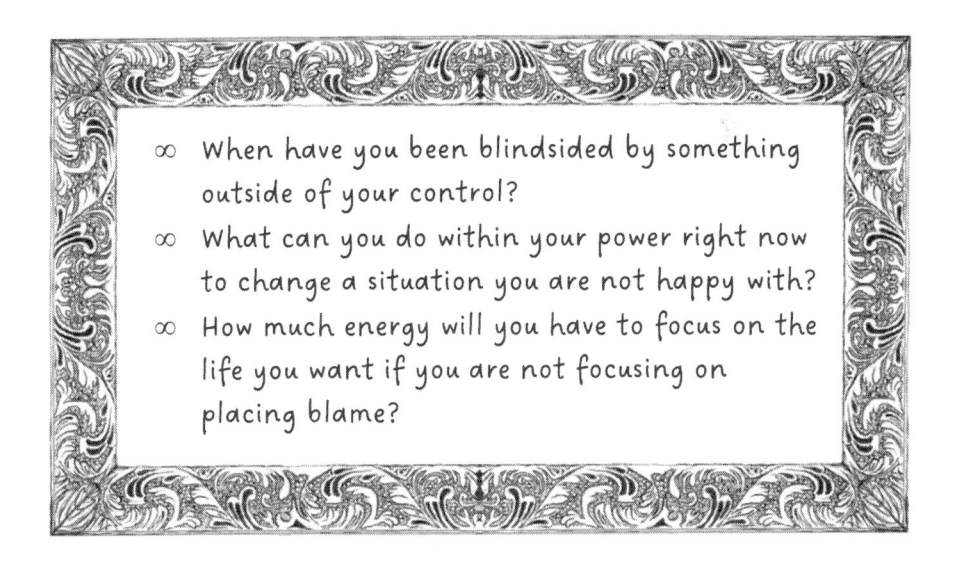

- ∞ When have you been blindsided by something outside of your control?
- ∞ What can you do within your power right now to change a situation you are not happy with?
- ∞ How much energy will you have to focus on the life you want if you are not focusing on placing blame?

Sometimes you board the ride before you even know the final destination.

You hesitate.

You're nervous, maybe even terrified. There's no guarantee.

But you're curious, so you step on-board.

You might have ideas in the back of your head of where you hope it leads, and where you really hope it doesn't take you. But you set those aside for the moment.

You start to move forward as it carries you from where you've been.

Is that okay?

Who are you leaving behind? You wonder for a moment before understanding there is no guarantee they would stick around anyway.

So you allow it to take you.

Will you ever come back? No.

Sure, you may revisit the same place or do the same thing, but it will never truly be the same again.

What lies ahead?

Anything. Everything.

Someday the ride takes you to an amazing new place you would never have chosen.

Sometimes it puts you next to someone you come to love who you'd have never met otherwise.

And sometimes you miss the best parts of the ride because you're so focused on where you want it to take you, that can't see where you are now.

We are all on the ride my friends.

Stay open.

Enjoy the view.

Love the other passengers.

And know that no matter where it takes you, the journey is always better when you are open to an adventure.

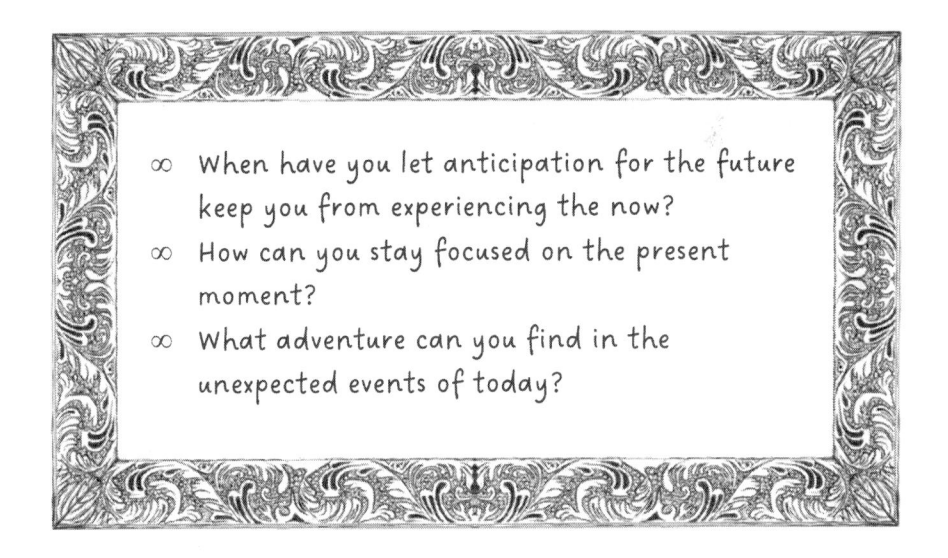

- ∞ When have you let anticipation for the future keep you from experiencing the now?
- ∞ How can you stay focused on the present moment?
- ∞ What adventure can you find in the unexpected events of today?

Sometimes your world is frozen. Time stops. Nothing seems to move forward.

You sit and take it in as you view the motionless world around you. Even the sounds of nature seem dampened by the weight of the freeze.

Your mind still races on as if nothing has changed. But eventually it too slows to match the pace of the scene you are in.

There you sit.

A rush of white noise fills your head as you strain to hear your own thoughts amidst a painfully loud silence.

Finally, they start to work their way in.

Things you haven't heard for a long time. Thoughts buried deep below the rush of your busy life. Ideas repressed by false priorities that now seem arbitrary.

Suddenly the frozen world is no longer the cold place you felt closing in around you.

Signs of life seem to scurry along the edges of the scenery. You can even hear the life again. It was always there. But now you have stopped long enough to take it all in.

You needed the freeze. You didn't know it, but you did.

It's grounded you again. Brought you back to the roots of your deepest thoughts. You appreciate the freeze.

You never thought you'd say this, but you don't want it to go away. But it will thaw, and the noise will reenter.

Though it's up to you my friend to keep your ears open and your mind focused.

As the world warms up, and the bustle of chores starts moving, choose to remember this moment.

To recreate it whenever you can. To not forget the little noises in life which you let get buried in the importance of nothingness.

For even in the busiest of days the frozen silence is still there somewhere. You just have to find it.

Enjoy the moment my friend. Find your peace.

And in the silence may you find the sound of your voice telling you just how awesome you are.

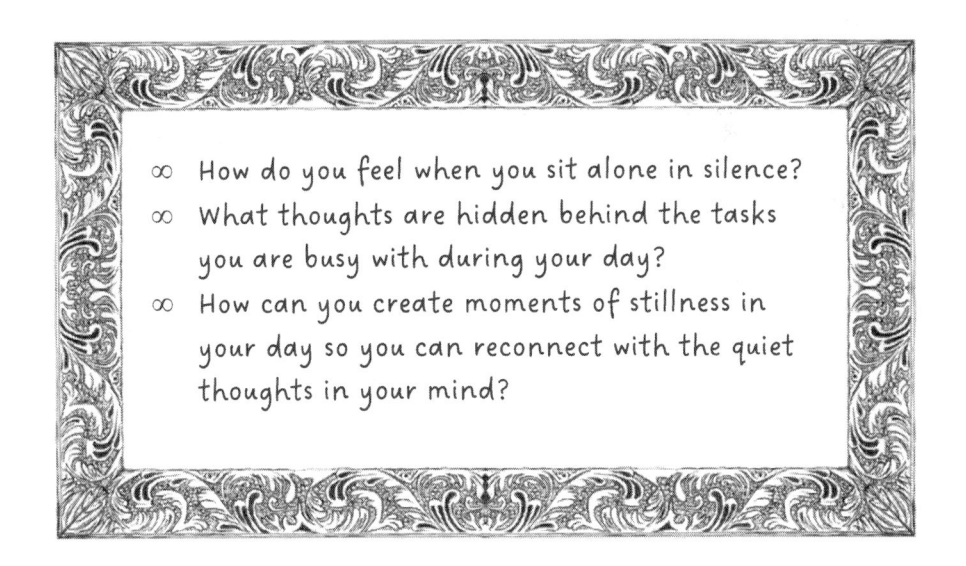

- ∞ How do you feel when you sit alone in silence?
- ∞ What thoughts are hidden behind the tasks you are busy with during your day?
- ∞ How can you create moments of stillness in your day so you can reconnect with the quiet thoughts in your mind?

Sometimes you wander through your city streets in the moment when night kisses the morning.

You notice the life hidden by the bustle of daily chores.

You look to your right to see a gleaming window in a luxury apartment. You think to yourself, people actually live here. You start to wonder who could live such a life.

How did they get to this place in the world? What course brought them here? Do they even know how different their life is?

You think to yourself, I could be there in just a few steps.

Then you look the other way. You see a row of tents lining the border of the park.

As the bitter cold seems to bite harder on your exposed skin, you find yourself once again having the same thoughts. You think to yourself, people actually live here. You start to wonder who could live such a life.

How did they get to this place in the world? What course brought them here? Do they even know how different their life is?

You think to yourself, I could be there in just a few steps.

You pause for a moment as you take in the very different worlds colliding in your path. You have a sense of guilty comfort knowing you are just a few blocks away from a warm bed.

Suddenly the life of luxury seems a bit less important as you find a renewed appreciation for the simple comforts of life.

And so you walk on. What did you just experience? How should you feel?

Aware. That is all my friend.

Aware that there are things to strive for. Aware that there are others struggling. Aware that you are just a few steps away from both lives.

Aware that no matter which path you take, you can help others along the way, but you can't take the steps for them. That is their own journey.

But all the while you can be aware that it will always be up to you, no matter where your path takes you, to make the biggest impact you can in this world.

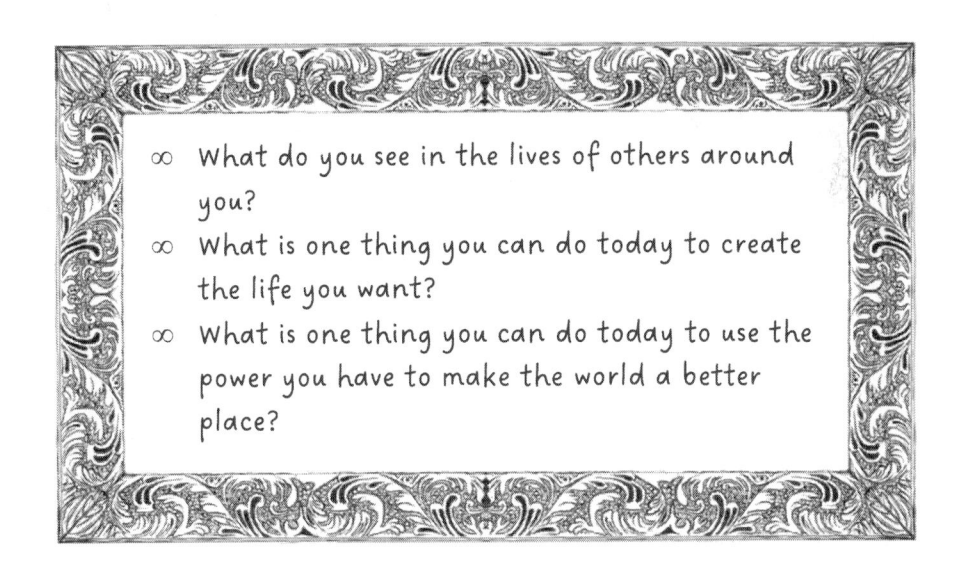

- ∞ What do you see in the lives of others around you?
- ∞ What is one thing you can do today to create the life you want?
- ∞ What is one thing you can do today to use the power you have to make the world a better place?

What is the best possible outcome of this situation?

Most often we are drawn to the negative. It's the first thing we notice. It's the only thing we can see. And we cannot see past it.

But if we pause and purposefully try to find the positive in a situation, we can see that there may be something there. By asking yourself what the best possible outcome could be, you tease your brain into acknowledging some form of positive exists.

The longer you ponder this question, the more time you spend in a positive landscape. You have just *turned the wheel*, if you will, in the direction you are driving your thoughts.

Sometimes you don't feel like yourself.

Something is off.

Or maybe it's spot on, and you're just not comfortable with it feeling that way.

So you sit in your discomfort.

You look to the outside world to try to pin this feeling on anything other than your own inner discontent.

There is nothing to blame. No person to point the finger at.

It's all on you. Or in you. Somewhere.

Are things going down the wrong path? Or are things going so well that you are entering territory you have never stepped foot in before?

Like stepping up a ladder one rung higher than you've ever been, your stomach churns with nerves.

Are you creating panic, because you need to feel inadequate? Do you crave the sense that life should always be a battle? Or is the ladder actually on unstable ground?

Just as the blame is not external, neither is the solution my friend.

The only way to solve this riddle is to quiet your mind, calm your senses, and to listen and to feel.

Only then can you find the source. Only then will you find the truth.

Only then will your heart be open to hear the answers you so desperately need.

Take time today my friend.

Don't let discomfort stop you from climbing higher than you ever thought possible.

But also, don't be in such a rush that you don't stop to let your mind hear your soul speaking to your heart.

And as you climb that ladder, take comfort in the fact that it will all feel better the longer you sit with the feelings of being higher up that ladder.

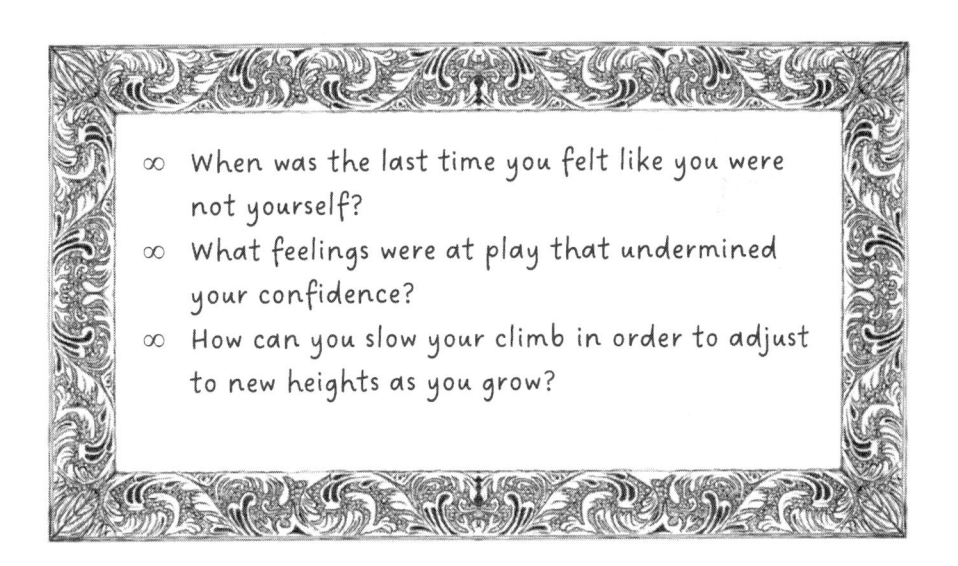

- ∞ When was the last time you felt like you were not yourself?
- ∞ What feelings were at play that undermined your confidence?
- ∞ How can you slow your climb in order to adjust to new heights as you grow?

Sometimes you feel high on life. Like nothing can go wrong. As if every hope you've ever dreamed is about to come true.

But that feeling goes away.

You sit in this place, absent of your high. Devoid of hope.

You try not to be dramatic, but you can't tell if the absence of the high means you're depressed, or if this is just normal and your expectations are unrealistic.

Whatever the reality is, it doesn't matter. Because the feelings are real. They are right there with you.

Even when you close your eyes, they don't go away. There's no escape.

So you sit with your feelings. The room is loud. Yet you hear nothing.

The sun sets, but you don't look up to see the beautiful colors.

You wonder, can you feel anything when you don't feel the high? Or is this just life? You're not in pain. There's just nothing there. Yet the absence is painful enough.

You yearn for feelings. For a presence. For that chance to see hope once again.

Then you give it some more thought.

You ask where you really are right now. What's the real problem here?

Nowhere. Nothing. It's just the absence that doesn't feel so great. But there's no real problem.

You know the hope will return. So you sit in the loud silence while you wait.

This is life. It's not all ups, and not all lulls are complete downs. But they are part of the cycle.

They give us a gauge for which to measure the height of the good times. They allow us to feel.

So when you're not feeling it my friend, just know that it's preparing you for good feelings to come.

That you are resting your hopes so they can live with vibrant excitement another day.

You're on the path to greatness even when you can't see the sunsets that lie ahead. But in this moment you just need to reframe the way you see it.

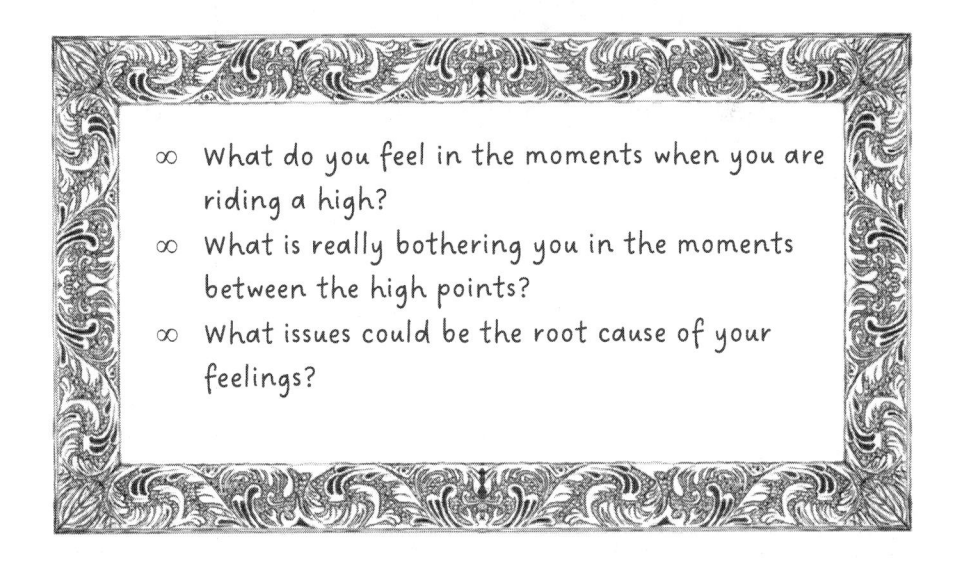

- ∞ What do you feel in the moments when you are riding a high?
- ∞ What is really bothering you in the moments between the high points?
- ∞ What issues could be the root cause of your feelings?

Sometimes you sit in a noisy world with silence inside your head.

You want to get lost in your own thoughts, but the distractions of trivial people seem to dominate the conversation in your mind.

You try not to listen. You really don't care. But their words bombard your defenses and invade the peace your mind would otherwise enjoy.

It's a test. And you're failing.

In your quest to find mindfulness, you find your thoughts are full of everyone else's mess.

You're doing it wrong. But not for a lack of trying.

Though just like trying to not think of something, the more you try to not hear them, the more they stay in the forefront of your attention.

Their words annoy you. Their tone bites your sensitive skin. But you can't find a safe harbor.

The noise seems closer now than ever before. It's no longer surrounding you. It's inside you.

Your once quiet mind has lost the battle and is now wrought with trivial words and phrases dumped there by the strangers whose only connection to you was to be within earshot.

But it's okay my friends.

The world is a crowded and noisy place. For in this hectic rage of sound there is life.
There is experience.

There is opportunity.

Opportunity to learn. Opportunity to grow. Opportunity to experience the life around you.

When the noise takes over, listen to the sound. Find a lesson and take it into the next stage of your journey.

That's life my friends. That's community. That's growth.
And it's all better part of the experiences which come together to form the amazing story of you.

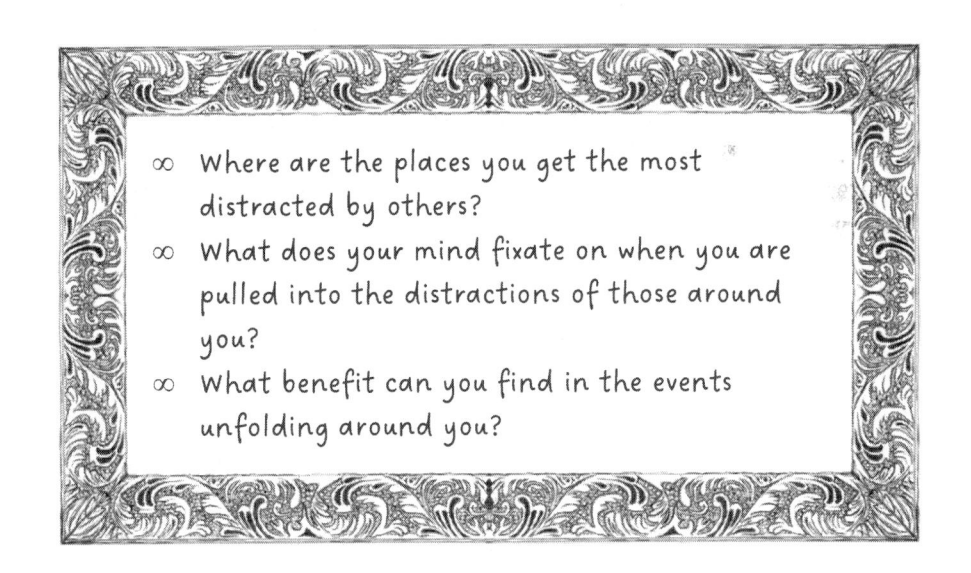

- ∞ Where are the places you get the most distracted by others?
- ∞ What does your mind fixate on when you are pulled into the distractions of those around you?
- ∞ What benefit can you find in the events unfolding around you?

Sometimes you have a plan for the day, or even for your life, and just like that something out of your control comes along and gets in the way.

You think about how you won't get to go wherever you wanted. You won't get to do the things you expected.

You might be disappointed and downright moping.

But that's just one way of thinking.

While you are looking out your window seeing only your perspective, there is an entirely different point of view at every vantage.

You pause a bit in your reflection as you become aware of the possibilities.

You notice that if you take just a half step in any direction, your perception shifts.

You are able to see that even though there are things which will never happen, there are even more things which can now happen like never before.

You let go of the plans you made. You move on.

You even begin to feel free from the expectations you'd chained yourself to.

You get excited about new possibilities you'd never considered or even imagined.

You're determined to take your renewed energy out into the world.

To dance in the snow.

To throw a snowball.

To make a snow angel.

To feel the crunch under your feet as you walk on a changed earth.

To leave your footprints behind as you journey forward on a new path.

When the world changes around you my friends you can make it amazing by shifting your perspective and reframing.

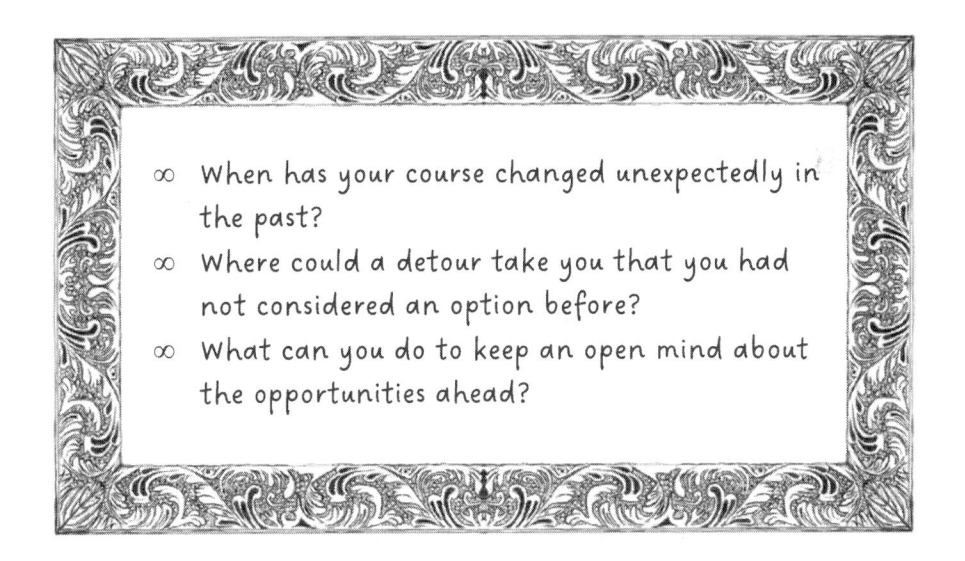

- ∞ When has your course changed unexpectedly in the past?
- ∞ Where could a detour take you that you had not considered an option before?
- ∞ What can you do to keep an open mind about the opportunities ahead?

Sometimes you find yourself awake in the time between late night and early morning in the space where dreams go on a date with reality.

You lay still, hoping to fall back to sleep until finally you accept the hard truth that your mind is more awake than your body is prepared to support.

Maybe it's close enough that you can start your day ahead of schedule. It feels like it could be.

You hold out from looking at the clock as long as possible. Until finally you break down and peek. No, it's way too early to begin the day.

You're stuck in that place where days don't exist. Where days are ending for some and starting for others, but not for you. You are meant to be asleep. But you're not.

Something crept into your mind and planted a seed to pull you from your slumber.

Maybe it was the hum of a passing car, a dog barking in the neighbor's yard, or a dream that felt so real you thought you were already awake.

Whatever the reason, here you are, wondering if yesterday needs to end or tomorrow needs to begin.

Time is frozen.

But your thoughts race forward.

Where are they going in such a hurry?

Will time catch up to the ideas flashing through your mind.

Will you even remember what they were when tomorrow decides to start.

You want to sleep. To silence the roar of thoughts. But you can't.

Eventually you do. There's no telling when or how, but finally you drift off as reality gives way to the world of your dreams.

You know when you wake back up, you won't know where the lines were between awake and asleep, conscious and subconscious.

All you know is that they mingled for a brief time in that space between yesterday and tomorrow that no one can really define.

As you drift off again you have one last thought: that no matter what tomorrow brings you're going to make the most of it.

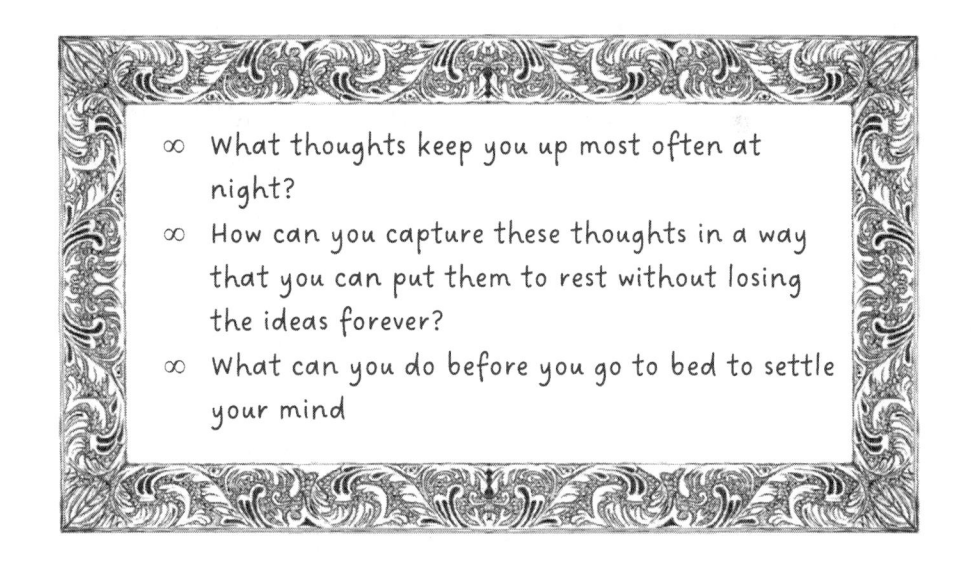

- ∞ What thoughts keep you up most often at night?
- ∞ How can you capture these thoughts in a way that you can put them to rest without losing the ideas forever?
- ∞ What can you do before you go to bed to settle your mind

Sometimes you look out into a world so grey, you can't tell where the water ends and the fog touches down.

It's dismal.

It's isolating.

It's overwhelming.

You don't know what's out there. What's beyond the fog. Or what could be hidden in the haze itself.

You sit with your thoughts as you contemplate the unknown.

There's fear and anxiety fostered in the fog.

Yet, it's peaceful, comforting, and calming at the same time.

You begin to see the grey as an empty canvas. An opportunity to move into the unknown without expectation.

This is freeing. In fact, you've never felt so free before.

You start to enjoy the fog. What you once viewed as a suppressor now feels more like its only purpose is to protect you.

You don't want the veil lifted now that you know it's shielding you from anything and everything that could come your way.

But the good news is the fog won't vanish instantly. It takes time.

It fades slowly as it gradually let's more sun under the covers.

Easing you out of your comfort zone and into the brightness of the world ever so delicately.

Enjoy the space you're in my friend, for the world is ever changing.

Like the fog staying around just for a time, so are the circumstances of our lives.

Keep your eyes open as new things come into view. As they enter your life, be ready to make the most of it as you shift into your new reality.

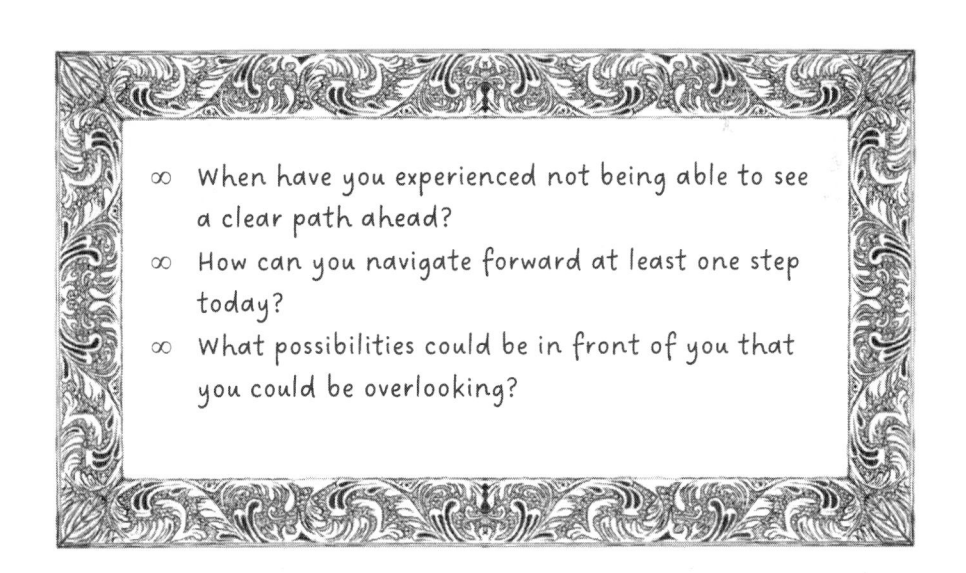

- ∞ When have you experienced not being able to see a clear path ahead?
- ∞ How can you navigate forward at least one step today?
- ∞ What possibilities could be in front of you that you could be overlooking?

Sometimes you put all your cards on the table.

You've tried playing it safe in the past. You've held your cards close to your chest.

But that hasn't worked out so well for you.

So now, you decide it's time to step out.

You figure it's the only way to play the game. Letting your whole self be seen.

But the other players don't play by the same rules.

You're confused. You're hurt.

You feel taken advantage of.

You wonder if you will ever win. You don't know if you even want to play another hand.

But you're not ready to quit the game altogether.

Then you look around at the other players.

Perhaps for the first time ever, you realize you're not playing at the right table.

You can't change the way you play to fit those around you who make up their own rules.

You can't give up because of one bad hand.

You need to find people who play on your level.

People who respect the moves you make.

People who call your bluff and show their own cards.

You step back from the table and feel relief. Noticing for the first time that other games are being played at different tables all around you.

You aren't limited to those who you happened to be sitting next to just by chance.

You can still be vulnerable my friend, and it will be reciprocated, when you play at the right table.

Just give it time and keep playing the game.

And while you play, keep your eyes open for just the right opportunity to lay your cards on the table.

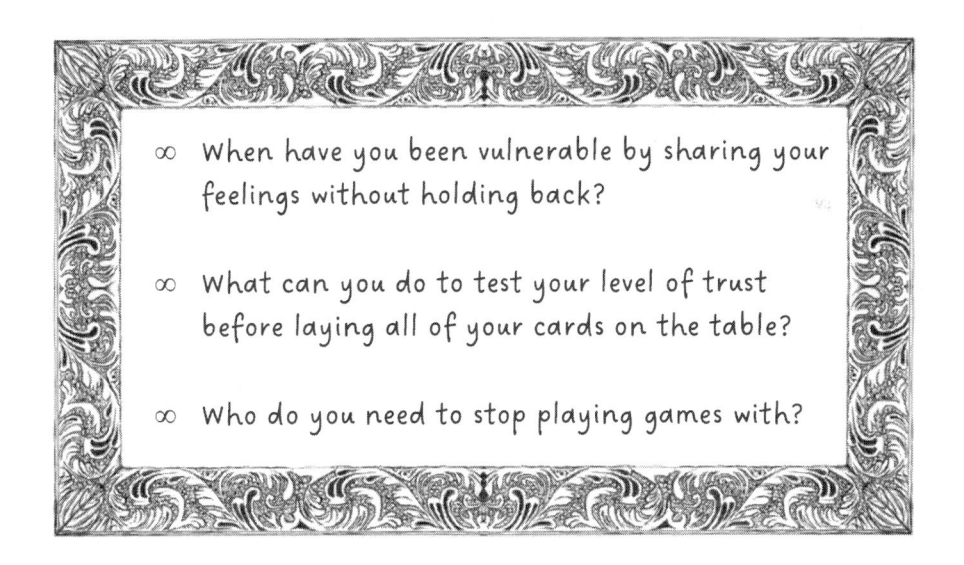

- ∞ When have you been vulnerable by sharing your feelings without holding back?

- ∞ What can you do to test your level of trust before laying all of your cards on the table?

- ∞ Who do you need to stop playing games with?

Sometimes you walk down a city street late at night and you wonder what's next.

Which path should you take?

Should you stumble into the next bar and try to make a midnight friend?

Should you follow the calls of the social scene?

Or should you head home and maybe search for a stroke of creativity in the quiet of an urban night.

Should you burn the midnight oil working on your next big thing?

Either could be the right answer.

Some nights one answer might seem more logical than another, while a different choice may tempt your heart.

So you stand on the street and feel the cold breeze taunting the back of your exposed neck.

Which direction is the wind blowing tonight? It's subtle, yet firm. It pushes you with the force of a feather sweeping against your skin.

You know you can resist. You know you can take control.

But you convince yourself, you don't have a choice.

Maybe it's what you really want: to take that step towards the other choice. But you justify it by blaming the breeze for sending you the way you choose.

It's okay my friends. Your path doesn't have to be explained to anyone. As long as it truly is what you want, follow it.

Take the step.

Follow the urge.
Lean in.

For in those moments, life happens.

And when life happens, you are living like never before.

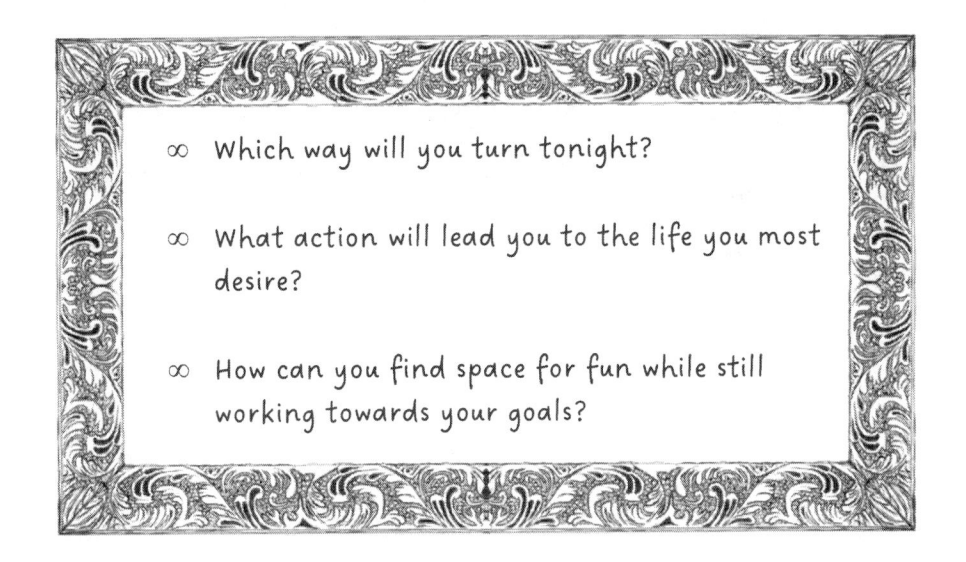

- ∞ Which way will you turn tonight?

- ∞ What action will lead you to the life you most desire?

- ∞ How can you find space for fun while still working towards your goals?

Sometimes you are seeking what you will never find.

You'll never find it because you don't really know what you want.

You think you do.

You tell yourself a bigger this will make you happy. Or a better that will solve all of your problems.

But when you find a bigger this, or a better that, you are left with the same unfulfilled emptiness in your heart.

So what can you do?

Practice being okay without.

For if you are okay without this thing, or those people, you will be just as happy when they do enter your life.

How do you practice being okay without?

Well, that comes down to gratitude. Take a few moments each day to list everything in your life you are grateful for.

A deep breath.

A song.

A pretty view.

A nutritious meal.

A smile from a stranger.

A moment in peace.

Once you spend time seeing all that you have, you will lose sight of the things you are without.

In this way you can learn to be happy without.

And it's only by being happy without that you can ever feel happy with.

You can hold space for accepting anything into your life, no matter how small.

You can look at it and find appreciation for all of the value it holds however small.

You can give up on waiting for the bigger this, or the better that, and say *this is good enough.*

Practice today my friend. And may it bring you peace through gratitude in all that you already have.

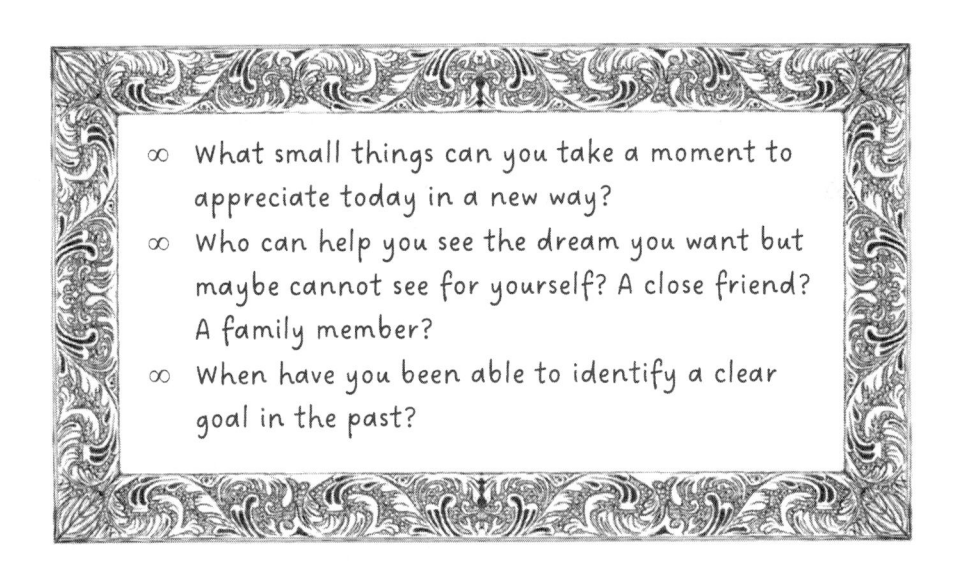

- ∞ What small things can you take a moment to appreciate today in a new way?
- ∞ Who can help you see the dream you want but maybe cannot see for yourself? A close friend? A family member?
- ∞ When have you been able to identify a clear goal in the past?

What would you tell someone else if they were going through this same thing?

We are often much kinder to others in their time of trial then we are to ourselves. If you can think objectively about what advice or words of support you would give to another, then you are one step closer to giving yourself an answer

If you struggle with where to start on answering this question, replace the words 'someone else' with any or all of these options: your best friend, your child, your parent, your sibling, a younger you, a stranger.

Thinking in this way helps pull the emotional ties out of your expectations surrounding the issue at hand.

Sometimes you meet someone who smells so good you just want to lean in.

You're drawn to them.

You don't know why. But something is pulling you closer and closer.

You hesitate.

You don't trust it.

You tell yourself it must be a trap.

It's too good to be true.

It's not just the smell. It's the smile. It's the look in their eyes. It's the ease in their voice. It's the charm in their personality.

You inch a little bit further into their influence.

You're testing the waters. Dipping a toe in to see if it feels comfortable or not.

It feels nice. You like it.

But you still aren't sure.

Why aren't you sure?

Is it something they've done or said?

Or, more likely, are they paying the price for the years of distrust you've curated from other past experiences?

Are they serving time for the crimes of others?

Yes. You know they are.

You're torn between the hard lessons you've learned from your past loves and the possibility that this is the one.

So you settle for a brief chat and a hope that chance will bring you back together again.

Maybe it will. Maybe it won't.

Either way, you're moving forward.

Every experience is a step in the right direction.

A practice for the big dance.

A chance to learn. To be more comfortable.

To prepare for the day you are ready to fully lean in.

For the day when your heart will be ready to once again accept the love you deserve.

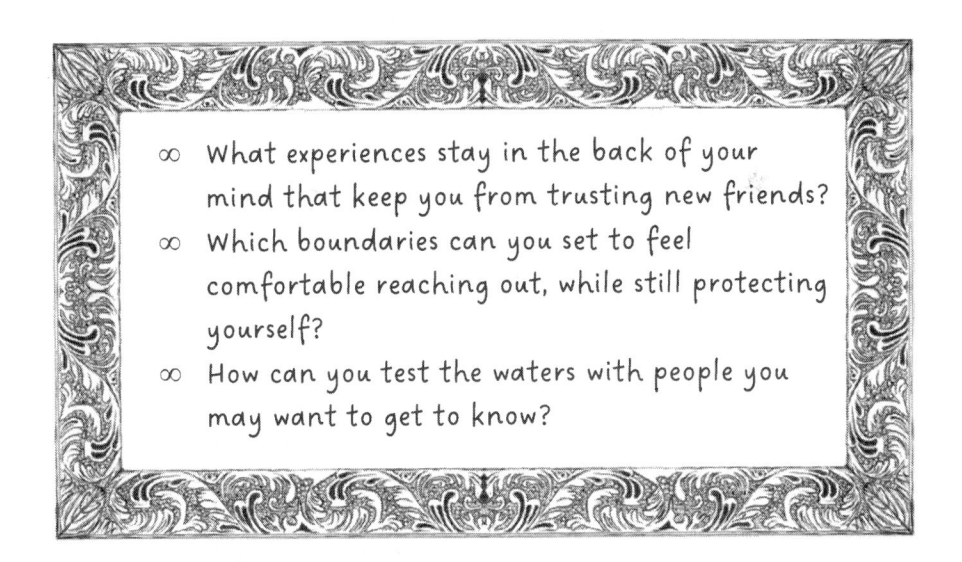

- ∞ What experiences stay in the back of your mind that keep you from trusting new friends?
- ∞ Which boundaries can you set to feel comfortable reaching out, while still protecting yourself?
- ∞ How can you test the waters with people you may want to get to know?

Sometimes you find yourself in a weird headspace.

You can't quite put your finger on it. But something feels different.

Maybe it's bad. Maybe it's good. You can't tell. Either way it's weird.

You think on it for a moment.

You close your eyes to drown out the sounds the city is forcing into your head.

You pause.

You reflect.

It's weird. Yet you can't tell if this is a good weird or a bad weird.

Either way you start to come to terms with the idea that weird doesn't necessarily have to be assigned to either trait.

Weird. Different. Abnormal. Unusual.

Who says any of those things have to be better or worse than regular, normal, or standard.

So you're in a weird headspace.

It feels different. It has you wondering.
But that's all it is for now.

A chance to think differently. To open up your eyes. To see new possibilities.

To find the opportunities hidden in the weird you've never explored before.

Suddenly it doesn't feel so bad to be in this headspace
you're living in at the moment.

In fact it brings you a new sense of hope. A chance at peace.

It's different and that's okay my friend.

Don't jump to conclusions about shade that difference could be.

Sit in the moment. Embrace the weird. And know that ...

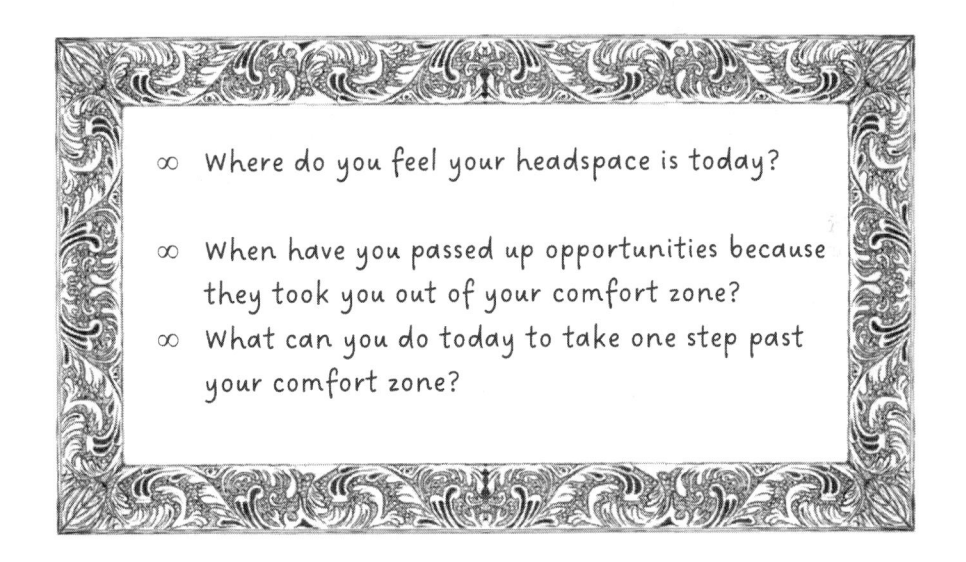

- ∞ Where do you feel your headspace is today?
- ∞ When have you passed up opportunities because they took you out of your comfort zone?
- ∞ What can you do today to take one step past your comfort zone?

Sometimes you notice the first signs of change happening around you.

They are subtle. A changing color. A few less leaves on the tree. A degree or two cooler. A few minutes less of the sun shining.

Yet you pick up on them just the same.

If you weren't paying attention you'd miss them entirely.

You'd be distracted by the things that haven't yet changed around you.

You'd tell yourself fall wasn't coming because the sun is still singing today.

You'd decide it isn't cold enough for a season to change.

You'd still see the green in the other trees around you who have not yet caught up to the mood change.

You'd live in denial that change could happen at all, because you have not yet seen enough evidence that it has already started.

But not today.

Today you've seen it. And it can't be unseen.

Like a truth you'd rather not know, you can't un-know what is now filling up the crevasses of your mind.

But it doesn't have to be such a bad thing.
Knowing gives you the chance to get ahead of the big changes ahead. It gives you the chance to decide for yourself while you have more time to make an impact.

You see the change coming. It doesn't have to scare you my friend.

Use this knowledge to your advantage.

Take the strategic lead to prepare for the change to come.
To know the days of now are numbered.

To appreciate the time left in this reality. While taking steps to make the most out of the next.

Change is always happening. Watch for the signs and don't be afraid when they start to show up.

Embrace the change and own it.

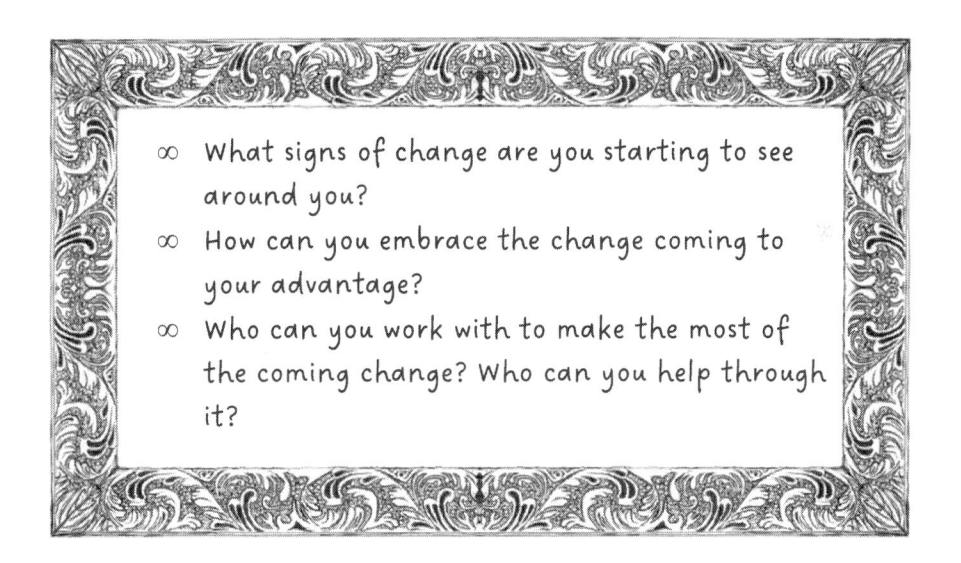

- ∞ What signs of change are you starting to see around you?
- ∞ How can you embrace the change coming to your advantage?
- ∞ Who can you work with to make the most of the coming change? Who can you help through it?

Sometimes you lie in bed as the day starts around you.

The hum of traffic passing by outside your open summer window tells you people are starting their days.

The slam of the neighbor's door as they rush out, late again. A dog barks. A bird chirps. Even nature is getting going. Yet you lay. Listening to the busy life just outside of reach.

Racing even faster than the late commuters, are the thoughts in your mind: your to-do list, your plans, your hopes, your dreams. All waiting for you to take that first step.

But in what direction will it be? Which dream will you walk towards today?

There are so many. And taking a step towards one, so often feels like walking away from another.

So you lay still. Looking for the answer. Hoping for inspiration.

Then in almost silence you find your peace.

In slowing yourself and pausing the rush in your own mind, you find the answer: it doesn't matter what you walk away from, only what you are waking towards.

You begin to understand that not taking a step in any direction means none of your dreams will ever come true.

Wouldn't you rather have one come true than none at all?

So you take a step. A step in any direction. Any dream will do today. Tomorrow you will take another.

Day by day, step by step, you will make something amazing happen.

Before you know it you will be miles down the road looking back on your journey.

You'll be glad you decided to take that first step in whatever direction you chose.

For if you hadn't, you would still be in the very same place you are today.

So take that step my friend. And know that with every step you take, you are doing one more thing to build your dream.

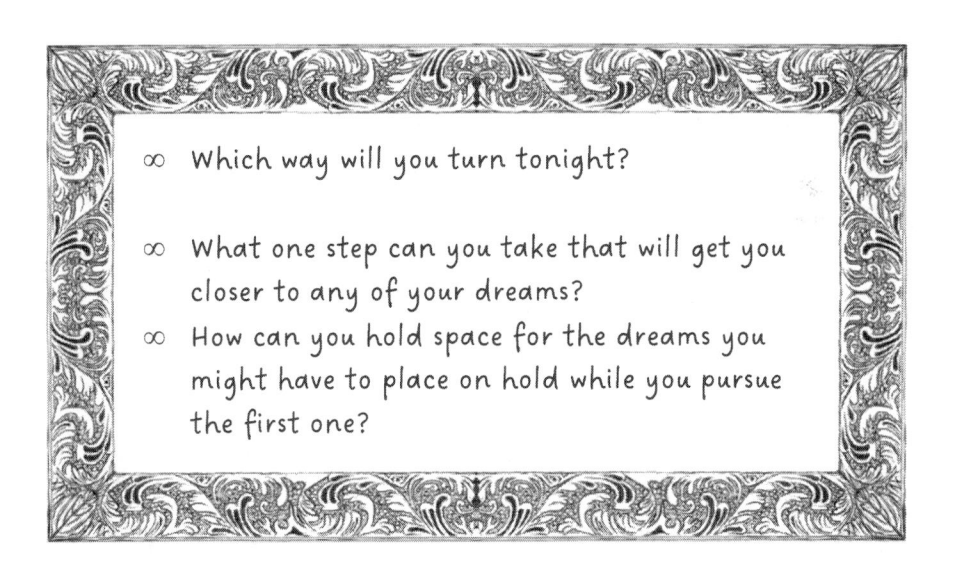

∞ Which way will you turn tonight?

∞ What one step can you take that will get you closer to any of your dreams?

∞ How can you hold space for the dreams you might have to place on hold while you pursue the first one?

Sometimes you sit alone and exposed in the world feeling small.

You see all the big trees around you. You just know they will always block you from feeling the sun for yourself.

They got their first. They planted their roots so deep there isn't any room for you. They've soaked up all the good water, leaving you fending for yourself trying to find your way.

You sit in this space and feel hopeless.

You don't even try to seek out other possibilities. You're so set in your mindset that you don't consider any other explanation for your situation.

That's where you can choose to stay. But you don't have to my friend. You can choose to see it a different way.

You can consider the journey of the other trees.
How did they got started?

You imagine the beginning of their growth. They were once just as small as you.

You begin to understand, as small as you are now, you already hold all the potential to be great.

You were born with it. It's sitting inside you waiting for you to let it out.

You just need to apply your determination and give it time.

Time for you to stretch out just enough to feel the first rays of sun nurturing your leaves.

Time for you to claim your space in the ground and find water of your own.

The sun will shine. It will reach you.

The rain will fall. It will feed you.

The seasons will change. They will strengthen you.

Time will pass. And you will be great.

And when you are, you can look down at the saplings and seeds on the ground wondering if they will ever be as big as you.

You can share your wisdom. Tell them yes. Share your story. And make sure they know, like you right now, they already hold all the potential for greatness inside them.

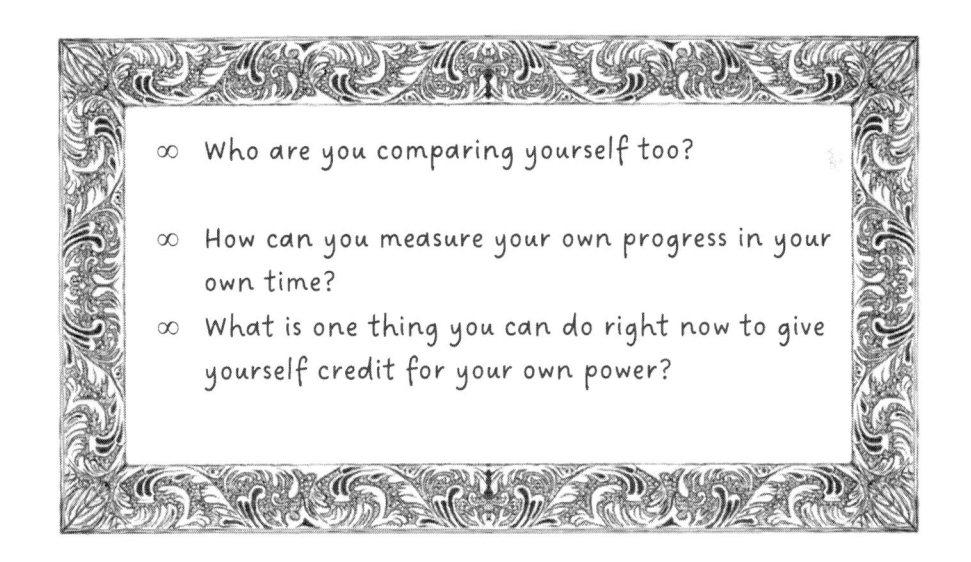

- ∞ Who are you comparing yourself too?
- ∞ How can you measure your own progress in your own time?
- ∞ What is one thing you can do right now to give yourself credit for your own power?

Sometimes you stop, frozen in your tracks.

You take a moment to look at the path before you and it's terrifying.

Obstacles seem to be closing in from all sides. The light is blocked out so you can't see a clear way through.

How will you make it through? Can you find your way?

There you are.

Stuck.

Needing to take a step, but you don't know if you have the courage.

The path ahead is scary. But scarier yet is the thought of never again moving forward from where you are.

You stand with the companionship of your thoughts until you decide it's time to move forward.

So you take a step in faith that you're going the right direction. You take a step in faith that you will make it through. You take a step in faith that you can do it.

A single step that changes everything.

They say the first step is the hardest. Stop believing them.

Change the way you look at it.

Tell yourself the first step is the most important.
It takes you from one reality into another. It brings you from fear and powerlessness into action and empowerment.

After the first step the rest will be easier.

Once you've taken this step, there is no going back.

Once you start moving, you know it will be ever forward.

And ever forward is the way you need to move in order to create the life you desire.

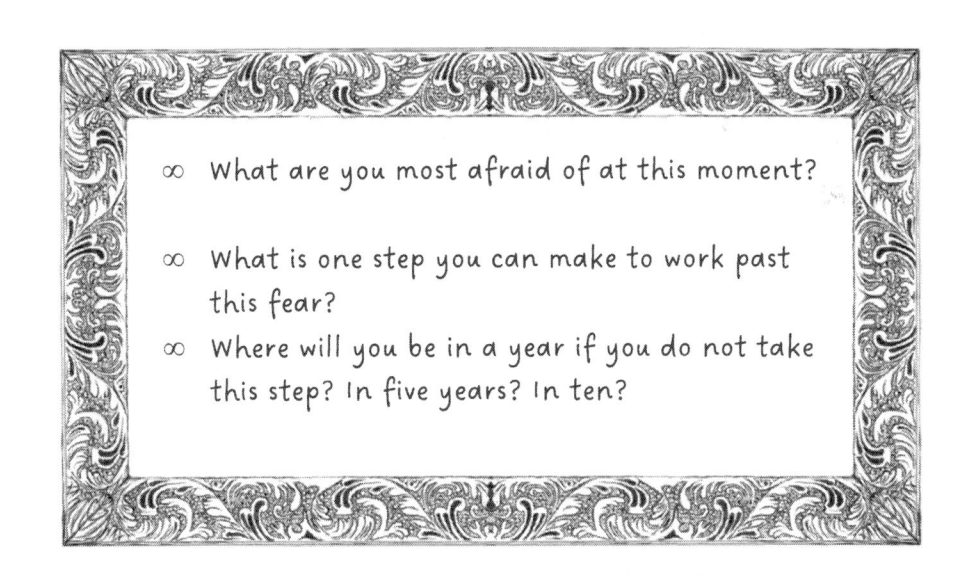

- ∞ What are you most afraid of at this moment?
- ∞ What is one step you can make to work past this fear?
- ∞ Where will you be in a year if you do not take this step? In five years? In ten?

Sometimes you don't notice when a good thing is starting.

When then light is shining brighter. When the nights are getting shorter.

But it's happening.

It's hardest to see at the beginning. The change is small. Just another minute or two of light. But it's there.

It's growing.

It's happening.

You just have to trust that it will continue. You have to stay focused on the little bits that are getting better every day.

You can see it if you look for it.

Sometimes you aren't paying attention. You miss it all together.

Until one day, when you suddenly look back and realize that there is more light in your world than there was before.

It will seem like it snuck up on you. But it was there the whole time, growing slowly in the shadows.

All the while you felt like the darkness would never end.

Dark nights will grow shorter.

Light days will grow longer.

Things will get better and better for you my friend.
Believe it.

Know it.

Look for the signs.

Watch for the hope.

And you will flourish my friend in the end.

All because, as the light grew, you were able to keep the faith and you were paying attention.

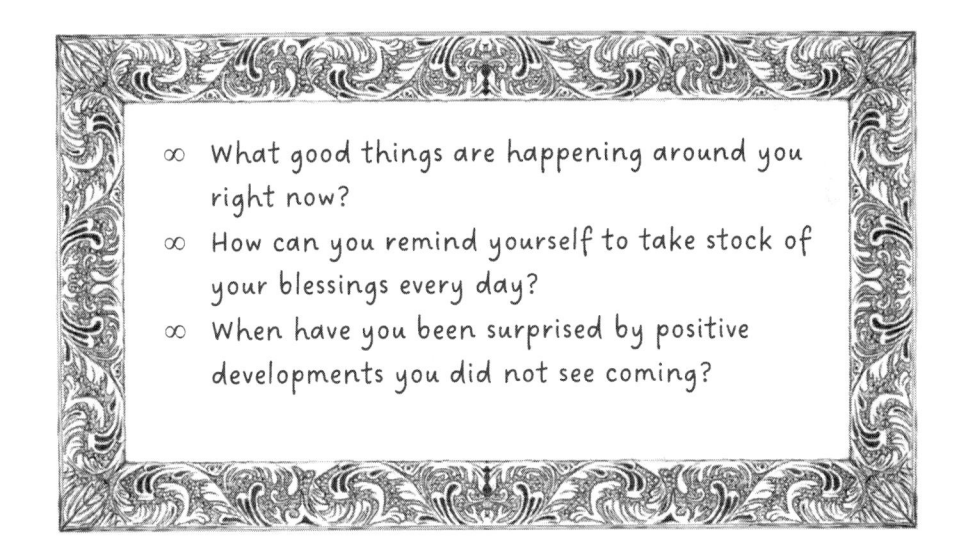

- ∞ What good things are happening around you right now?
- ∞ How can you remind yourself to take stock of your blessings every day?
- ∞ When have you been surprised by positive developments you did not see coming?

Sometimes you think you read it right.

You were sure you caught the feels.

You were riding high on the hope of a new adventure. A chance to live like never before.

But then you look again to see you had it wrong.

The vibes you thought were for you were not sent in your direction at all.

You jumped in front of a bullet that wasn't aimed at you. And it swerved hard to miss you.

You feel foolish. You feel embarrassed.

The hope you felt lifted you just high enough to make the fall that much further from the ground. That much more painful.

So now you lay on the pavement.

Feelings crushed.

Pride bruised.

No longer trusting your intuition.

You wonder, should you retreat to your lonely habits?

Will you find solace in the lies you tell yourself that happiness hides in your distractions?

Will you care to ever try to love again?
But then you think about the life you live and the dreams you have waiting for you.

You remember how big your dreams are and that they are bigger than the attention any one person could give you.

You think of the love you have from so many even though none of them come home with you at the end of the night.

You find determination in moving forward towards that dream you've been building for so long.

And you think that just maybe somewhere along the way someone special might fit into that life.

But if they don't, it's pretty amazing just the same.

Once again peace enters your mind and consoles your heart.

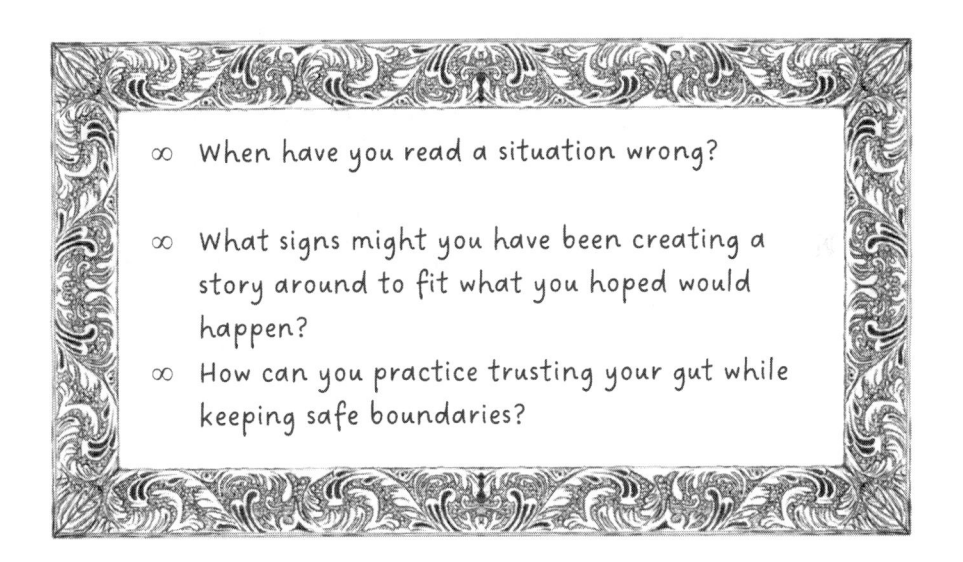

- ∞ When have you read a situation wrong?
- ∞ What signs might you have been creating a story around to fit what you hoped would happen?
- ∞ How can you practice trusting your gut while keeping safe boundaries?

Sometimes you make a decision only to later wonder what you were thinking.

It seemed right in the moment.

But when the dust settles you can't help but think it wasn't the right choice.

There is no amount of justification that can prove you were of sound mind. But it doesn't really matter.

The choice was made. The decision chosen.

So you go on with life.

You may not understand what you were thinking in the moment. Even though it was you.

You can't blame anyone else.

It was you.

You don't know what to do now so you do the only thing you can do.

You accept it and move on.

There are times my friend when we don't make the right choice. When we look back and say, "If only I had more time. If only I thought that through."

But that's not life.

Life is full of emotional responses. Of knee-jerk reactions.
Of things we "should've" thought through. But the choice was made. The actions taken. And we can't take it back.

You can, however, take a moment to just accept it. And live your best life my friend.

Do you.

Accept that bad choices have been made.

Learn from them.

Make note of what you will do different the next time. Choose better when you are given the chance.

Life is about learning, growing, and improving.

Live in the journey and love the growth.

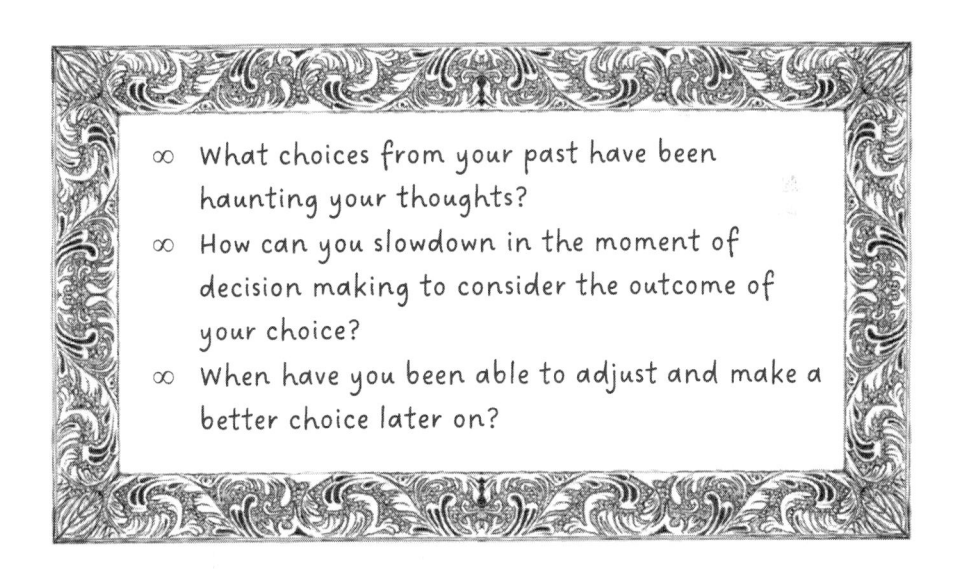

- ∞ What choices from your past have been haunting your thoughts?
- ∞ How can you slowdown in the moment of decision making to consider the outcome of your choice?
- ∞ When have you been able to adjust and make a better choice later on?

When have you felt like this in the past and made it through just fine?

The most important part of this question is the last five words. We often get caught up in how we feel, but we forget to pay attention to the fact that we have made it through okay.

Acknowledging both aspects, that you have felt this way before, and that you turned out okay, helps relieve the pressure of a looming bad result. It brings you out of the doom and gloom thinking.

You might not know where this situation will take you in the end. But understanding that your current feelings do not dictate the result will ease some pressure.

Sometimes you stare at a blank canvas with so much creativity inside you. But you don't know which mark to make first.

So the canvas remains blank. You sit. You stare.

Your mind wanders from idea to idea as you cross them off the list of options.

All the while, the canvas lays before you awaiting the impact you will make.

It seems so pure. You hate to make the wrong move.

You do not want to diminish its value by putting anything less than your very best out there for the world to see.

So the canvas stays blank. The world does not get to see anything you could do.

It's in this moment that you gain a better understanding of the canvas. Of its purpose.

The canvas is meant to be marked up. To be used as a catalyst for your expression. Even when it is not yet perfect.

It's meant to be the playground for your dreams. The place where your ideas are tried and expressed.

The blank canvas has no value. Its value is given by the marks you place on it. The perfectly planned strokes, as well as the wrong moves.

So you decide to start making your mark. You pick up the brush and make moves.

Some feel like a good start. Others are horrific mistakes.

But all are there in front of you building into a beautiful masterpiece right before your eyes.

So my friend, don't be afraid to dirty the canvas.

Don't hold back your talents from the rest of the world to see.

Paint that picture. Write that poem. Do that thing.

Appreciate the masterpiece that is unfolding on the canvas of your life as you find your way.

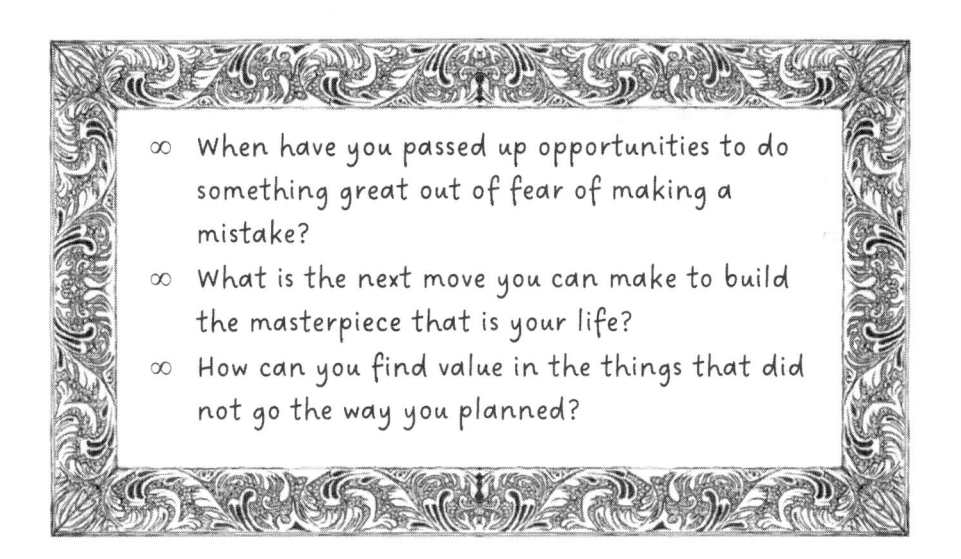

- ∞ When have you passed up opportunities to do something great out of fear of making a mistake?
- ∞ What is the next move you can make to build the masterpiece that is your life?
- ∞ How can you find value in the things that did not go the way you planned?

Sometimes you notice the sunrise like you never have before.

You start to see how much it relates to your own success.

Before you feel it, you sit in the dark.

You don't know if you can trust that it will grace you with anything special. Maybe it will leave you in the cold dark of night yearning for its light and beauty.

Only those with the fortitude to last the darkest hours will see the glow of success begin to crest over the horizon.

Then it begins. You see the glimmer of light.

The world softens around you as the colors change and the mood is set for a beautiful day filled with glorious things.

But it's fleeting.

This moment of perfect colors and peace soon give way to the hustle of a world that awakens around you.

The beauty of the moment is gone. You quickly learn that it is not enough to simply make it through the night.

Once the sun has risen you must now face the danger of the light. Looking directly at success feels dangerous, like the naked sun.

It burns.

It blinds.

It shows every exposed part of you.

Now you must have the fortitude to sit in the light of day without the shelter of the dark.

Can you make it through until sunset when nature will ease your mind with a lullaby of colors?

Setting you gently down to rest as she says to you, "You've made it, now rest well for another night."

You reflect again on the sunset and how it relates to your own success.

For the first time you understand that success is an ongoing process, an adventure, a journey. It is not a destination to reach and never move past.

Stay alert my friend. For in your pursuit of success, you are creating it. Success is happening every step of the way.

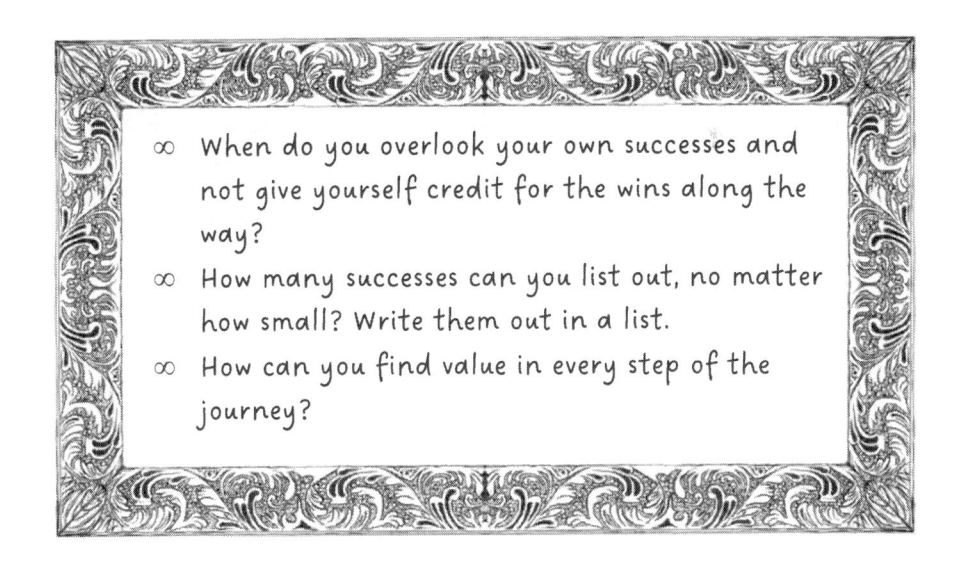

- ∞ When do you overlook your own successes and not give yourself credit for the wins along the way?
- ∞ How many successes can you list out, no matter how small? Write them out in a list.
- ∞ How can you find value in every step of the journey?

Sometimes you sit in a crowded place and feel invisible.

You're surrounded by people meeting friends while you sit alone in a corner.

Your ears are filled with the chatter of happy reunions and the taunt of laughter from jokes you weren't meant to hear.

You long to hear the sound of your name, but it won't be uttered in this crowd.

Your eyes take in the faces who seem to look past you as you dare them to make eye contact.

You are here, aren't you?

Can people see you?

Could you really be invisible?

You wonder, while your mind wanders to places you don't want to admit you've visited.

And here you sit in a crowded room, yet all alone.

But it's okay.

You're not the only one alone.

Masked by the noise, and hidden by the crowd, there are others.

You take another look around and see that this room has more than just your corner.

Tucked away, quietly in different corners, almost invisible, are others just like you.

Hoping to be seen. Feeling as overlooked as you.

Yet you see them.

They are no longer invisible.

You have the power to help others be seen.

To walk up to them.

To ask their name.

To be alone together.

You can be the voice who says their name which they thought, like you, they would never hear in this crowd.

As you approach, and ask their name, you see their smile and the noisy crowd fades from view as you share a joke the others were not meant to hear.

When you feel alone, know that you are not the only one.

In that, you will find the power to change the world, one smile at a time.

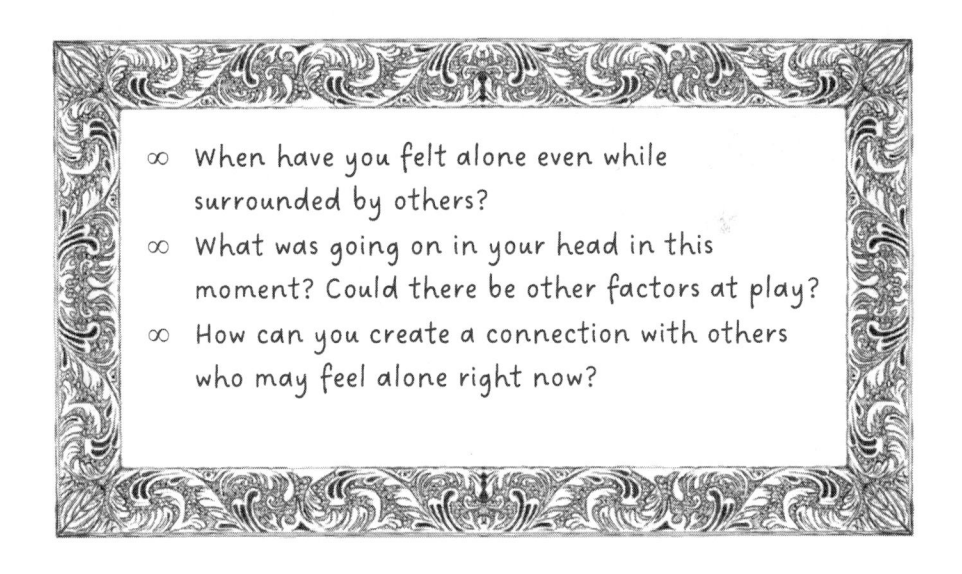

- ∞ When have you felt alone even while surrounded by others?
- ∞ What was going on in your head in this moment? Could there be other factors at play?
- ∞ How can you create a connection with others who may feel alone right now?

Sometimes you know what you want.

You might not want to admit it.

Admitting you want it means doing something about it. It means taking action to make it come true.

You don't want to do that. Well, maybe you do, but you are afraid to.

You probably won't acknowledge that it is your fear keeping you from pursuing it.

It feels better to make an excuse. To justify your own procrastination with lame stories you convince yourself to believe.

But deep down you know.

You see it.

You fantasize about it.

But you turn your head when it gets too close.

Maybe it's a person. Maybe it's an opportunity. Maybe it's just something fun.

But either way, you live your life without it, because, well, it's just easier that way.

You fool yourself by saying you're happier living life this way.

In reality, you're taking the easy road and accepting less for yourself.

But how would life feel if you really accepted what you deserve?

What experiences might await you?

My hope for you my friend is that you find your worth.

That you accept your value and nothing less.

And that you allow that amazing thing into your life which you really want.

You deserve it.

You're worth it.

Let the good things into your life, one small win at a time.

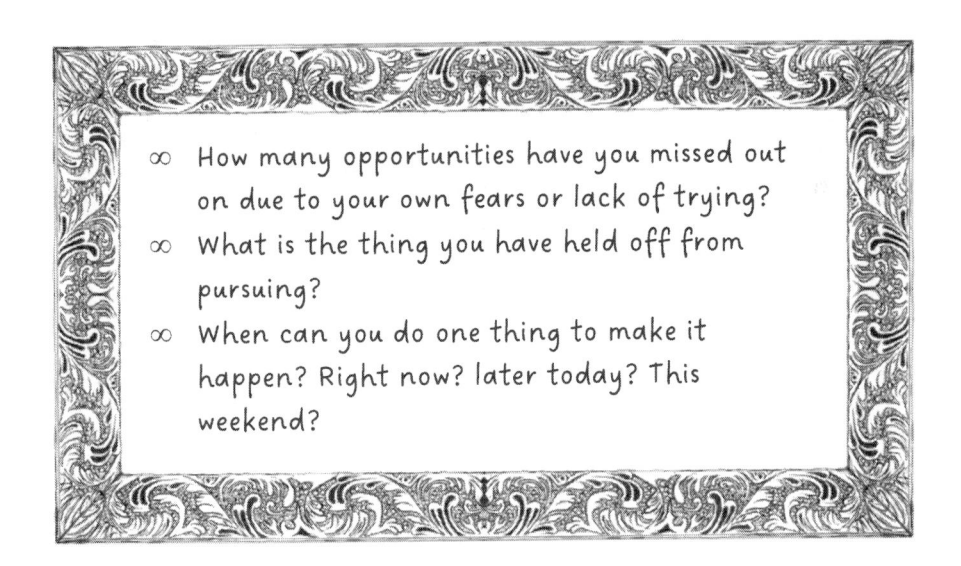

- ∞ How many opportunities have you missed out on due to your own fears or lack of trying?
- ∞ What is the thing you have held off from pursuing?
- ∞ When can you do one thing to make it happen? Right now? later today? This weekend?

Sometimes you end up at a late-night bar on a holiday evening.

You spend too much tipping the cook you've been crushing on, but don't have the courage to ask out.

You get a sultry kiss goodnight from a stranger.

It feels great, but you know he's not your type.

Even harsher, you know he has eyes for someone else.

Either way the short time together brings comfort. It hides the loneliness you both feel in the moment.

It's okay.

It is what it is.

You tell yourself you'll have courage another day.

Sometime soon, you'll ask him out. You'll ask if he likes you too.

You'll see if he even shops in your department.

But for tonight, you'll fall asleep knowing others feel the same way.

Knowing a stranger has the same feelings for another guy he's afraid to ask out.

You'll rest easy knowing in that moment you connected because you're both alone, but alone together. And in that loneliness the kiss was magical.
You could pretend it was meant to be, but in reality, it was only a place holder for the one you really want.

Yet in time my friends that one will see you.

They will want you.

They will seek you out.

On that day, the kiss you thought was so amazing will fade in comparison as you feel love like never before.

But first, you must truly be okay alone.

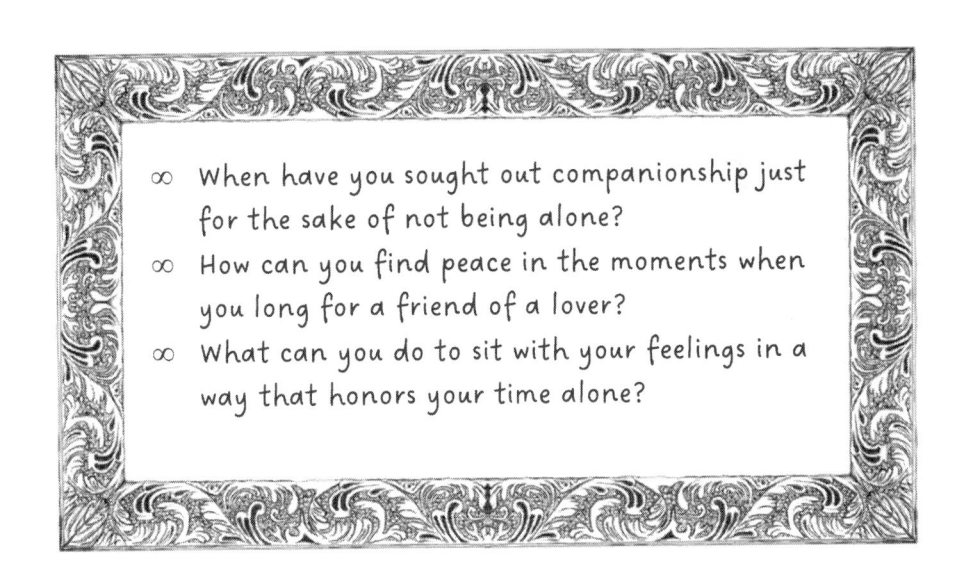

∞ When have you sought out companionship just for the sake of not being alone?
∞ How can you find peace in the moments when you long for a friend of a lover?
∞ What can you do to sit with your feelings in a way that honors your time alone?

Sometimes you just let life get away from you.

You follow a path, thinking you're being spontaneous, cool, or brave.

But in reality, you're just taking the easy choice. The safe bet. The easy road.

You're following. You're along for the ride in someone else's story.

It might be easy, but in the end it doesn't feel right. It's just not you.

You fake it for a long as you can. Though at some point you just can't be a follower anymore.

You need to bust out. You need to live your life. You need to be yourself.

So you leave.

You step outside.

It's cold at first. It's dark. It's scary.

You're downright terrified.

But there you are. Alone. Stepping out. Being you. Taking the lead. Doing your thing.

For the first time ever, you are stepping in the direction you want to go.

You've never felt so right.
The fear falls to the back of your mind.
Suddenly you are more in control of your destiny than you have ever been.

You have power. And you are using it.

You start to understand that you can take your life in any direction you want.

The monsters suddenly seem smaller.

The cold air has less of a bite to it.

For the first time ever, it seems doable alone.

All because you took a step outside and braved the world on your own terms.

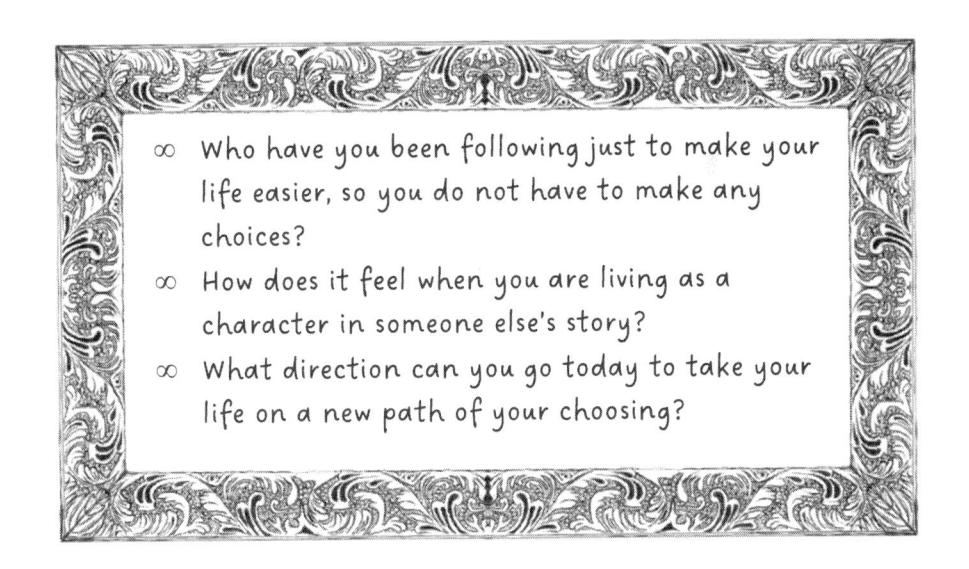

- ∞ Who have you been following just to make your life easier, so you do not have to make any choices?
- ∞ How does it feel when you are living as a character in someone else's story?
- ∞ What direction can you go today to take your life on a new path of your choosing?

What other factors could be at play affecting how you feel right now?

It is a commonly accepted concept that different people will not handle issues the same way. We all step into situations bringing a different combination of experiences to the event.

As true as this is, individually we might approach the same experience from a different mindset depending on our frame of mind in the moment. Traffic will stress you out a bit more when you already woke up late.

Practice looking outside of the issue to consider what else is going on in your life at the moment that could be contributing to your perception of the current situation.

Sometimes you've done everything you could be expected to do in a day.

You've plowed through your to-do list and even surprised yourself with just how much you could cram into one day.

Yet you lie in bed thinking there is more to be done.

Once out-of-reach dreams have started to visit you in your waking hours giving you a taste of what it's like when they start to come true.

They tease you with the hope that they could be a reality beyond your bedtime imaginings.

Yet you've done all you could today. And here you lie. Your still body trapping a mind that won't stop moving.

It's moving in every direction. Bouncing off the walls as it tries to do at least one thing more.

More planning. More solving. More creating. Anything more to push your dream forward.

Your dream is not patient. It will not wait for anyone. Not even you. If you can't keep up, will it leave you behind?

You wish you could bottle this energy and save it for another day.

Save it for one of those days when your enthusiasm and motivation is a far cry from the needs of your dream.

But that's not possible. Even the thought is giving your mind one more idea to solve which is keeping you up even later. Or is it?

So here you are. With a mind that won't stop. And the hope of not losing the power it holds in this moment.

The only way to satisfy your brain is to let it be heard. Capture those thoughts and ideas.

Grab a pen. Flip on the light. Open the notebook. And let your brain speak.

Let it share every thought it can. Let every idea flow as fast as you can write it out. Don't let the smallest voice go unheard.

You'll give yourself a whole new list of ideas to work on in the moments when the ideas aren't flowing.

You'll let the voice inside your head be heard. You'll tell your dream that it won't be set aside.

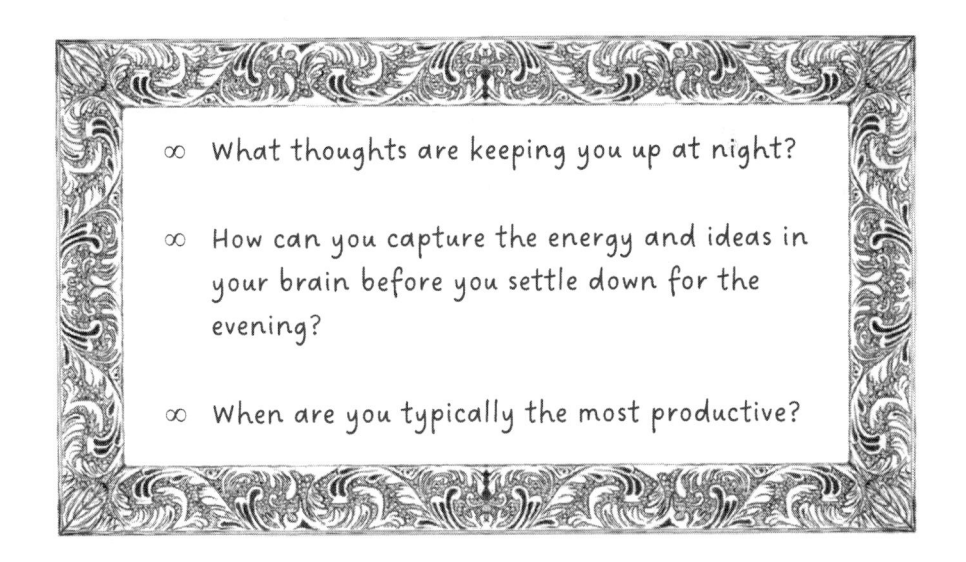

- ∞ What thoughts are keeping you up at night?
- ∞ How can you capture the energy and ideas in your brain before you settle down for the evening?
- ∞ When are you typically the most productive?

Sometimes you get to sleep in as long as you want.

You don't have to get up and clock in.

You don't have to race out the door.

No one is waiting on you to show up. No one is left disappointed that you didn't get more done.

You lay in bed and think, "I don't have to meet any deadlines today." So you feel justified laying there a bit longer.

And then you think about your dream. There is no deadline on that.

It can take a day or a decade to come true. Either could be okay. But not for you.

Suddenly feeling justified while living with an unrealized dream doesn't seem like a trade-off you can live with.

So you jump out of bed and get the day started.

Sure, you can sleep in.

Sure, you can justify it all day long. But that won't make your dream happen.

Sure, no one is waiting to see how long it will take. No one that is, except for you.

Yes, there may be days when you need the rest. When there is value in sleeping in.
Embrace those days.

Then, on the other days, the mornings where you don't need to recharge, start your day as soon as you can.

Start your dream as soon as you can.

You can be justified. You can deserve a break.

You also deserve your dream.

It's on the way, one early start at a time.

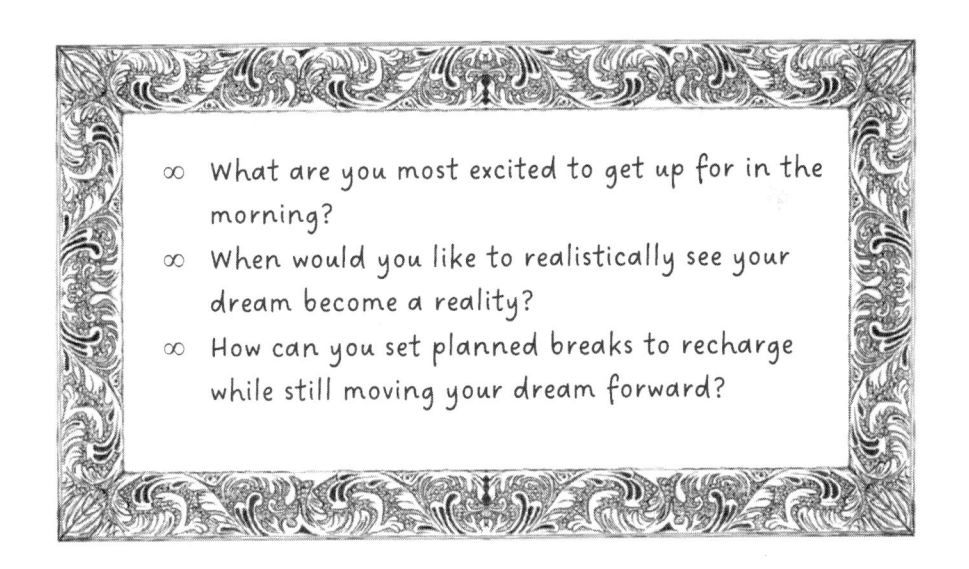

- ∞ What are you most excited to get up for in the morning?
- ∞ When would you like to realistically see your dream become a reality?
- ∞ How can you set planned breaks to recharge while still moving your dream forward?

Sometimes you wonder where the streets of your city will lead you.

Will you find a cafe, meet a stranger and get lost in an endless conversation? Will you do something you've never done before?

Or will you turn a corner and wind up with the wrong crowd?

Maybe you won't go very far at all and just experience the same neighborhood on an endless loop.

The streets can take you anywhere. The combinations of different routes are endless. Even a dead end can lead you to an adventure you will never forget.

Or they can hold you captive.

You rejoice when the streets take you where you want to go. You thank them for the places you have seen along the way.

You blame the streets on the days they keep you from your dreams, saying to yourself, you'd have the life you want if only the streets would take you where you want to go.

Everything is because of the streets.

Or is it?

You think a little deeper and start to question if the street is only a small part of your fate.

Life, after all, is the sum of all parts of a great equation built upon many different factors. Maybe the streets are just one small part of the problem. Perhaps you have more control thank you knew.

You look down at your feet with a new perspective and start to wonder where you want them to take you.

Where could you go if the streets lead anywhere you desire? What will you seek out? Who will you encounter along the way?

Now, look again and notice your feet, moving along the avenue.

Feel a sense of empowerment knowing that no matter where a street might lead you can take a step in a different direction at any moment along the journey.

You can detour down a side road, hop on the interstate, and fly past the things you don't want to hold you back.

This is both satisfying and serves as a warning. For no matter where you expect your street to go, one simple step can alter that for better or for worse.

So today, my friend, take a few steps down a road you are excited to explore. And know that you may find another road on a different day.

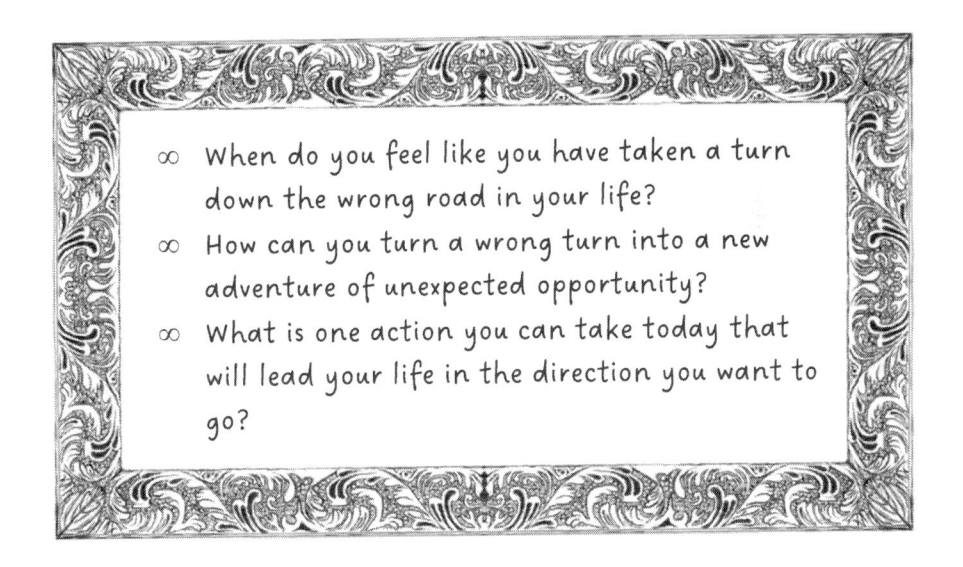

- ∞ When do you feel like you have taken a turn down the wrong road in your life?
- ∞ How can you turn a wrong turn into a new adventure of unexpected opportunity?
- ∞ What is one action you can take today that will lead your life in the direction you want to go?

Sometimes you get stuck in the weeds.

You can't seem to take a step in any direction towards where you want to go.

You fight to get out.

But your struggles are for not.

For every action you take, every kick, every stroke, only brings the weeds in closer to you.

You're in a tangled mess.

The more you try to fight your way out, the further you seem to sink.

What is this place you have ended up in?

Is it a jungle with a quicksand floor?

Can you ever move past this and get to solid ground?

Can you find a place where your feet will support your body and the vines won't strangle the breath out of your dreams?

Yes. Yes, you will.

There is hope.

The weeds will let go. The ground will become stable.

You will walk with security and trust in your surroundings once again.
But only after you surrender.

Sometimes it is not in the fighting to get away, that you become free, but in the stopping to reflect that you find your way out.

Once the splashing stops and the weeds loosen. You can come up for air.

You might even find that the weeds keeping you down are supporting beautiful life on the surface.

If only you dare to stop, to reflect, to take the time to see it.

The weeds are part of any garden, and not always what you think they are.

Pause. Reflect. And look for ways the weeds can help you get through the toughest times.

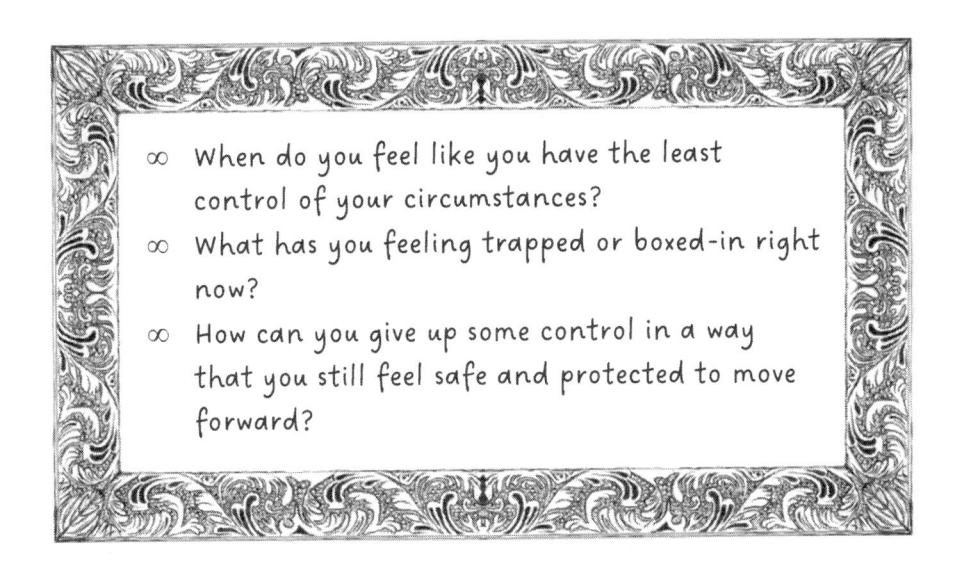

- ∞ When do you feel like you have the least control of your circumstances?
- ∞ What has you feeling trapped or boxed-in right now?
- ∞ How can you give up some control in a way that you still feel safe and protected to move forward?

Sometimes you have a big idea.

Something that will take your life to the next level.

Something that will fulfill your wildest dreams.

You have always wanted to hit it big, but you haven't known what to do.

Now finally, the idea is here in front of you, showing you the way.

Showing you just how to get to the life you want to be living.

But you do nothing.

You don't act on it.

You let the idea fade from your mind.

You tell yourself you're not ready. You decide to wait until you are big enough to be worthy of this dream.

You limit yourself solely by the thoughts you have. You decide to stay right where you are.

But why?

Why aren't you big enough? Who says you can't make it happen?

When will you ever be any more worthy than you already are?

It's all in your head: the timing, the limits, the lies.

It is time. Right now.

Now is the time to take that step. Build that dream.

Ignore the lies in your head.

You are worthy. You are ready.

You will make something big happen.

All you have to do right now is decide.

Decide to take the action.

No one else can take the action for you.

I cannot wait to see what steps you take today to create the amazing life you want.

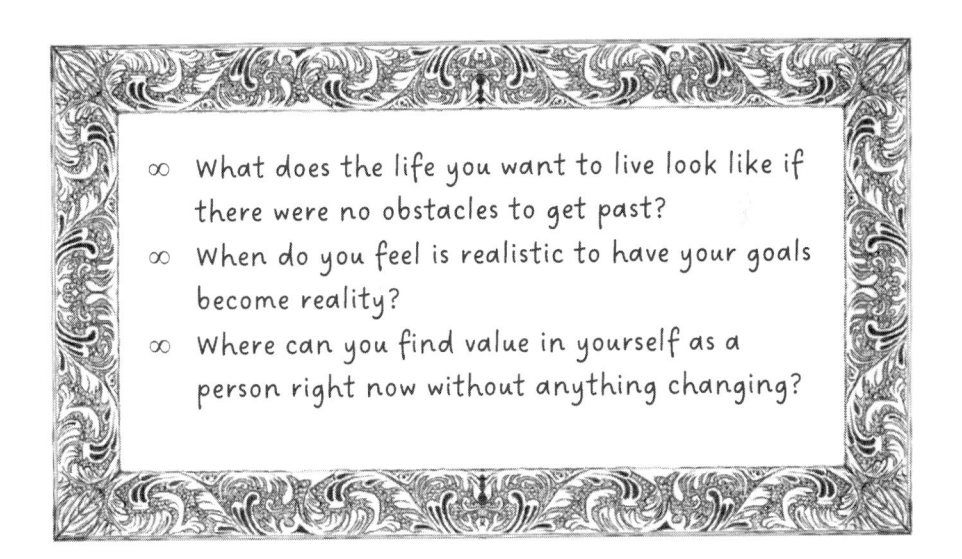

- ∞ What does the life you want to live look like if there were no obstacles to get past?
- ∞ When do you feel is realistic to have your goals become reality?
- ∞ Where can you find value in yourself as a person right now without anything changing?

Sometimes you have to take the leap. You have to jump further than you think is possible.

You don't want to. It's the scariest thing you have ever faced.

Your mind races with all the possibilities that could go wrong.

What if you trip when you start running?

What if you don't jump high enough?

What if you miss the landing?

How far will you fall then?

These things consume you as you sit on the opposite side of the canyon from the life you want to be living.

Separated only by your fears and insecurities.

While your mind taunts with all of the what-ifs, your heart interrupts with its own set of what-ifs.

What if you never jump?

What if you never even try?

What if this is all you ever dare to make in life?

In an instant you begin to understand. Both sets can be just as scary.

Both can lead you to a life you would rather not live.
In the end, the scariest option will push you to your choice.

Will you be more afraid to try and fail? Or will you be more afraid of the life you will have if you never try at all?

You know what you already have. You decide you want more.

So you know you have to take the leap.

In comes the courage you never knew you had. In comes the life you never dreamed you could experience.

All because one day, you took the big leap.

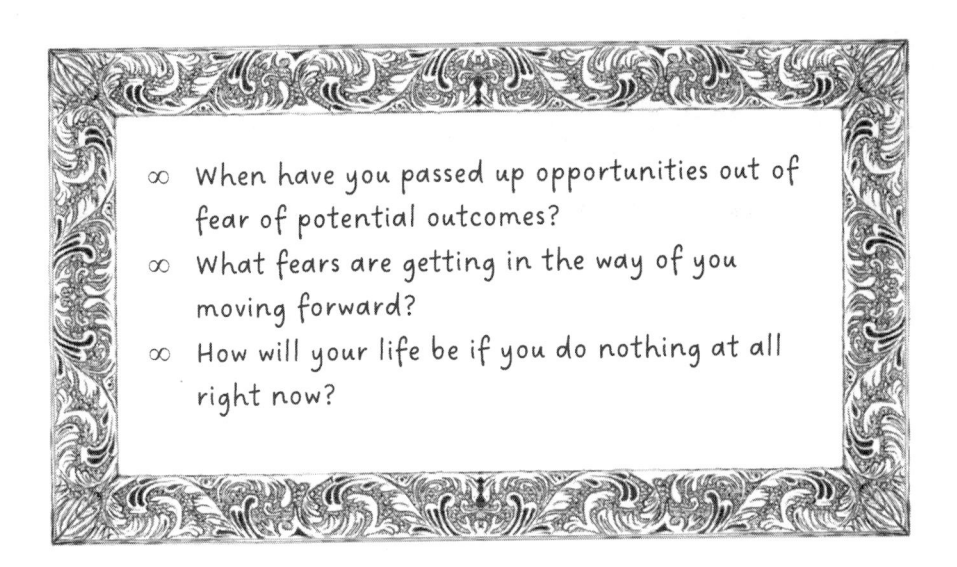

∞ When have you passed up opportunities out of fear of potential outcomes?
∞ What fears are getting in the way of you moving forward?
∞ How will your life be if you do nothing at all right now?

Sometimes you feel more exposed than you've ever felt in your life.

You were safe and protected in your own element until something changed.

Suddenly the blanket that covered you in a false sense of security vanished and gave way to the harsh mood of the air around you.

You freeze.

You tense up.

You cling to the only familiar thing still within reach.

Maybe if you stay put, the tide will rise and bring you back to the comfort of familiar waters.

But what if it doesn't?

How long can you hold on?

Who will see you in your most vulnerable state?

Will they help you, or will they take advantage of you?

You wonder if anyone has ever felt so alone.

They have. And they see you now.

They look at you hanging on with every bit of courage you can muster.

They see your beauty.
They hear your story.

They feel your pain.

They admire your strength.

They know that we all have those days.

Even though we aren't always here to witness when others experience them.

As you hang on, waiting for your world to get back to normal, they see you.

They admire your ability to shine even in your discomfort.

Don't dismiss the beauty you bring to the world even in the moments you can't see it for yourself.

It's in these moments that you have the ability to shine brighter than ever before my friend.

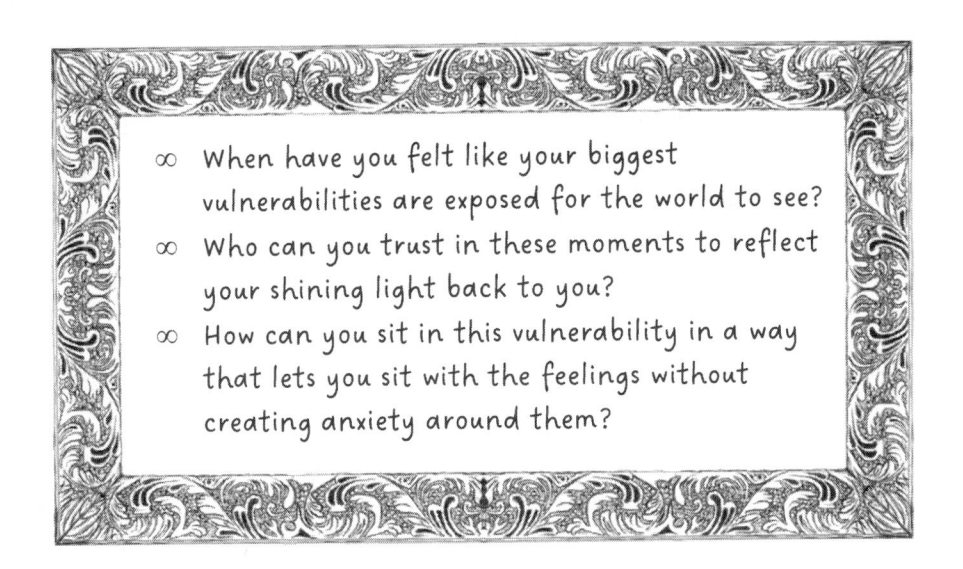

- ∞ When have you felt like your biggest vulnerabilities are exposed for the world to see?
- ∞ Who can you trust in these moments to reflect your shining light back to you?
- ∞ How can you sit in this vulnerability in a way that lets you sit with the feelings without creating anxiety around them?

Sometimes you are driving down the highway of life with your partner by your side.

They have been there for as long as you have known you existed.

You cannot remember life without them.

Then one day you pass an exit and they stay behind.

You drive along ,down the road without them, though you are not sure you will make it very far alone.

At first you don't move very fast.

You are sure you will run out of gas before another day turns to night.

You take your foot off the gas. But you don't stop.

You keep going.

Your journey seems slower for a time, but the road signs keep flashing past you as you move further down the road.

You're still moving along.

You don't know how. But you just keep going.

You can see their exit in your rear-view mirror.

It's right there. You can't look back without it blocking your view of any life in the before times.

They still seem so close. Like they could be in the car with you. Maybe just moved to the back seat.

You try to look forward, but the mirror is always in your sights and so are they.

You know you must move on, but it seems heartless to continue without them.

But the car won't stop.

And so you must move along.

As they would want you to do. As you would want them to do if the tables were turned.

A little further down the road, and their exit is getting smaller in your mirror.

It's there. You haven't forgotten about it. But it no longer blocks your view of the rest of your past travels.

The mirror stays in your view always. They stay in your mind always. But your journey is meant to continue.

You drive along with the memory of the happy days you spent riding together.

But you drive on as you know they would want you to do.

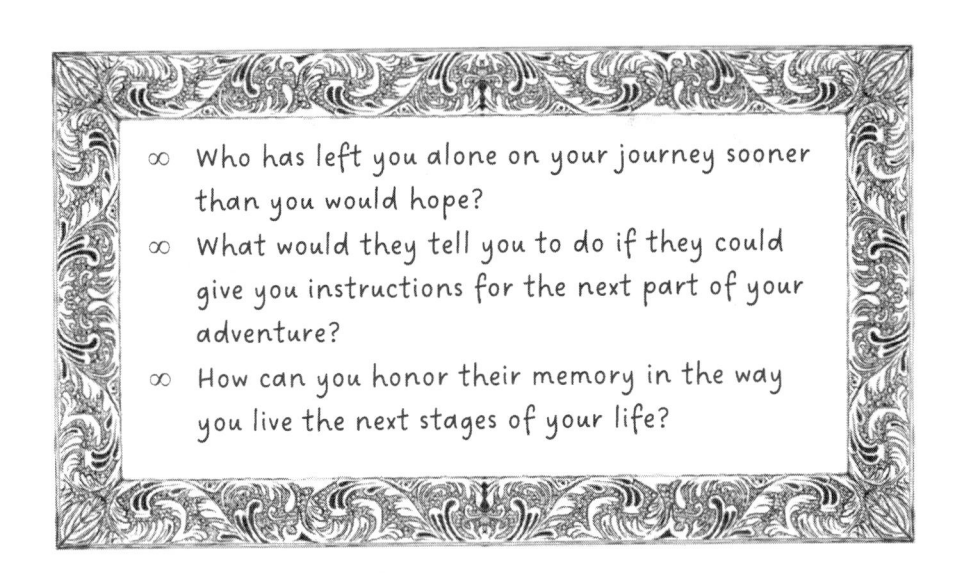

- ∞ Who has left you alone on your journey sooner than you would hope?
- ∞ What would they tell you to do if they could give you instructions for the next part of your adventure?
- ∞ How can you honor their memory in the way you live the next stages of your life?

Sometimes you try your hardest but you still don't win the game.

You pull everything together to make that last shot, but you miss.

Or maybe you made it, but the other team had already scored more than you.

You're exhausted.

You're spent. Physically and mentally.

Beyond that, even your spirit is gone.

What more could you have done?

Should you even keep trying the next time you are invited to play?

Yes.

Yes, you definitely should keep playing.

But you are playing the wrong opponent.

You need to understand who your biggest opponent really is.

You need to learn their tactics. You need to know their weaknesses.

You need to learn to play against them in a way that has them stunned by your competition.

But first you must acknowledge who they are.

Who is your biggest opponent?

You've been targeting the wrong one all this time.

You have not felt like you are not winning at this game because you are keeping score against the wrong team.

Perhaps the person you are competing with isn't the other team at all.

Maybe you have scored more points than you ever have in your life, but you don't celebrate the win because you compare your performance to the other guy.

You are missing your chance to take your victory lap to celebrate the growth and endurance you have made it through to.

Change the game to compete with a different opponent. Compete with yourself. With your past achievements.

Celebrate your wins. Congratulate yourself on your growth.

You are your own opponent and beating yesterday's version of you is the only victory that matters.

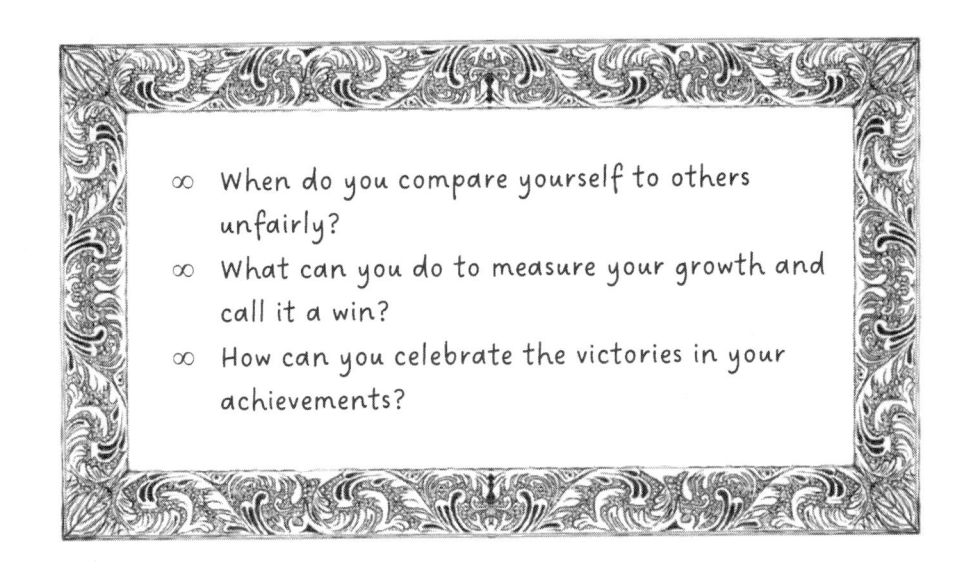

- ∞ When do you compare yourself to others unfairly?
- ∞ What can you do to measure your growth and call it a win?
- ∞ How can you celebrate the victories in your achievements?

97

How can you tell this story in a different way with a better ending?

We like to create stories to help our minds make sense of situations we encounter. How many times have you had half the facts and created a story to piece together what must have happened?

Your thoughts will do that before you even know they have taken over filling in the blanks. The challenge is for you to pick up the pen and become the author. Write the story in a different way.

You don't need to think of all the possible alternatives. As long as you can come up with one different story, you can then change your thinking from "this has to be the story" to "maybe there are other explanations."

Sometimes you lock eyes with a stranger so intense the connection takes hold and roots itself in your veins.

Time freezes yet the world spins around you in a frenzy as if you are in the eye of a hurricane.

There you stand in a moment you can't make sense out of.

Maybe it's in a coffee shop, maybe a bar, or perhaps in the checkout line at the store.

Wherever it is, you were not expecting it.

Should you look away and break the moment?

Should you stay locked in this dance?

Why are you feeling so connected?

With a chemistry you've never felt this stranger has rocked your world in less time than it would take to ask their name.

Then you wonder, what is their name? Are they also feeling the pause in reality that has you frozen?

Are you misreading the situation? Do they even shop in your department?

Should you dare to ask?

Why not?

Sometimes in the eye of the hurricane, you find peace and can make bold moves in the rare moment when you have the chance.

Other times survival mode kicks in and you run for cover while you can.

Either way, the eye passes.

The storm returns. And you never know what was carried away with it.

Be daring my friends.

Moments pass and are gone forever.

If you don't ask you will never know.

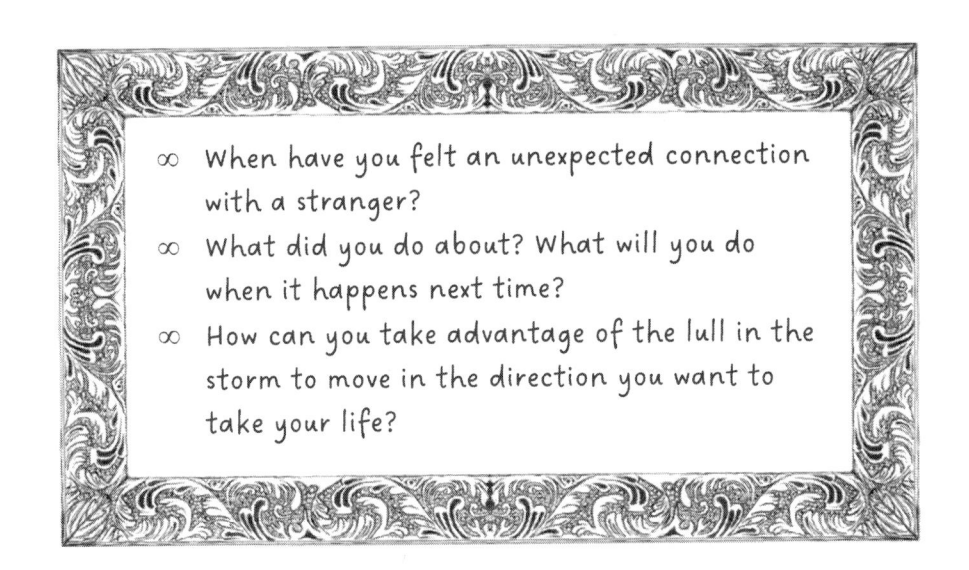

- ∞ When have you felt an unexpected connection with a stranger?
- ∞ What did you do about? What will you do when it happens next time?
- ∞ How can you take advantage of the lull in the storm to move in the direction you want to take your life?

Sometimes you look back at where you've been and it's hard to believe that was ever you.

You see a life you could never accept now.

You see a standard below what you're willing to allow.

For a moment, emotions set in.

Embarrassment for where you were.

Fear that you could end up back there.

Anger for the reason that kept you trapped for so long.

But the emotions only stay as long as you continue the conversation with them.

At some point you stop answering their plea. You say, I'm done with this conversation, and you walk away.

Away from fear.

Away from anger.

Away from resentment.

You join a new discussion. You choose to talk about the gratitude you feel.

Gratitude for the lessons you learned.

Gratitude for the people who helped you along the way.

Gratitude for the good things you were able to salvage from a broken life.

Gratitude for the life you have created from a new starting point.

Suddenly it's not embarrassing anymore.

It's not a sad dark part of you. But rather a darker time in your life that highlights the beauty of the brighter days you have ahead.

Just as the shadows on a sculpture highlight the beauty in every curve of a work of art, so do the dark moments in our lives give a backdrop to our best times.

Live in the bright moments my friend. Know they will come if they are not already here.

And when you step into the shadow, or when you think of a darker past, know those moments are only there to make the brighter days that much richer.

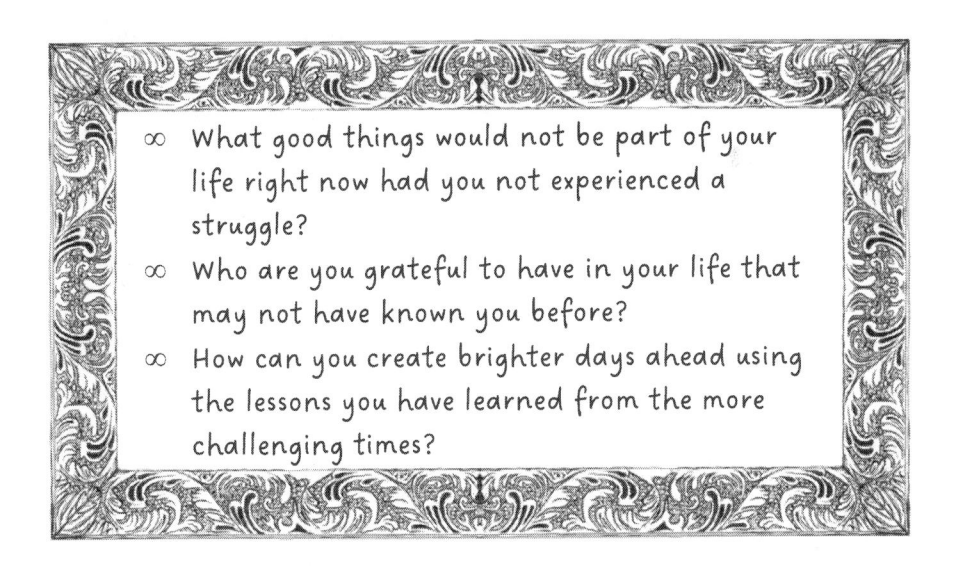

- ∞ What good things would not be part of your life right now had you not experienced a struggle?
- ∞ Who are you grateful to have in your life that may not have known you before?
- ∞ How can you create brighter days ahead using the lessons you have learned from the more challenging times?

Sometimes you can't seem to get your head in the game.

You try to get some work done. You tell yourself you will buckle down.

But you don't. You might strap yourself into the chair, but no work gets accomplished.

You are distracted.

Something good is coming and you cannot get your mind past the anticipation.

Or perhaps something scary is looming and fear is dominating your thoughts.

Whatever it is, it has control of your mind, you do not.

Yet you know there is work to be done.

There are things you want to cross off the list, but who can work with all of this going on?

You can.

You just have to set aside the thoughts and take control of your day.

The more you try to tell yourself to stop thinking about all the things, the more the things dominate your mind.

Stop. Pause. Breath slow.

Turn your mind the way you would steer your car around a corner, bringing your goal into the center of your vision.

See only your goal ahead of you at the end of the road you have just turned down.

Now slowly push down on the gas.

Move yourself a little closer to arriving.

Just do one thing, no matter how small, that will take you closer to your goal.

Tell yourself you can take another turn once you reach your destination if you need to come back to the distractions.

You can visit it, when it is time.

But you can decide when it gets to be a point of interest in your journey.

You are in control of whether or not it gets to be in the center of your vision rather than a blip of color in your sideview mirror.

Take control. Steer the car. And drive towards your dream my friend.

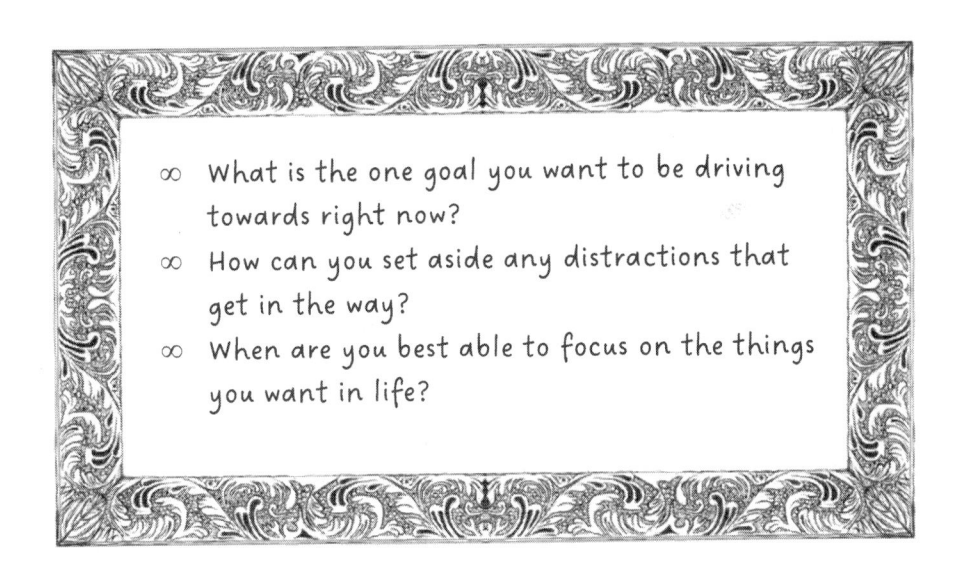

- ∞ What is the one goal you want to be driving towards right now?
- ∞ How can you set aside any distractions that get in the way?
- ∞ When are you best able to focus on the things you want in life?

Sometimes you randomly run into that person you couldn't get over.

You see them.

They look at you.

Suddenly a new thought comes to your mind.

You wonder what you were hung up on.

You try to see it. But it's just not there.

They bring in the charm. It pulls you in for a moment. Yet you're not fully hooked.

You ask yourself: what did I see in them?

You wonder why you had so many restless nights.

But the answer never comes.

You may just never know.

There they are in front of you, years later, with nothing pulling you in.

If you only knew that this was how they would end up.

That you would be so very okay without them.

If in those past moments, you could have known that they would now be so easy to overlook.

Would you have wasted a single minute on them?
Most likely not.

Here they are.

Here you are.

Times have changed.

All of the sudden nothing seems important about that moment you had five years ago.

You've moved on.

Though you never thought you would.

You did.

And you will again.

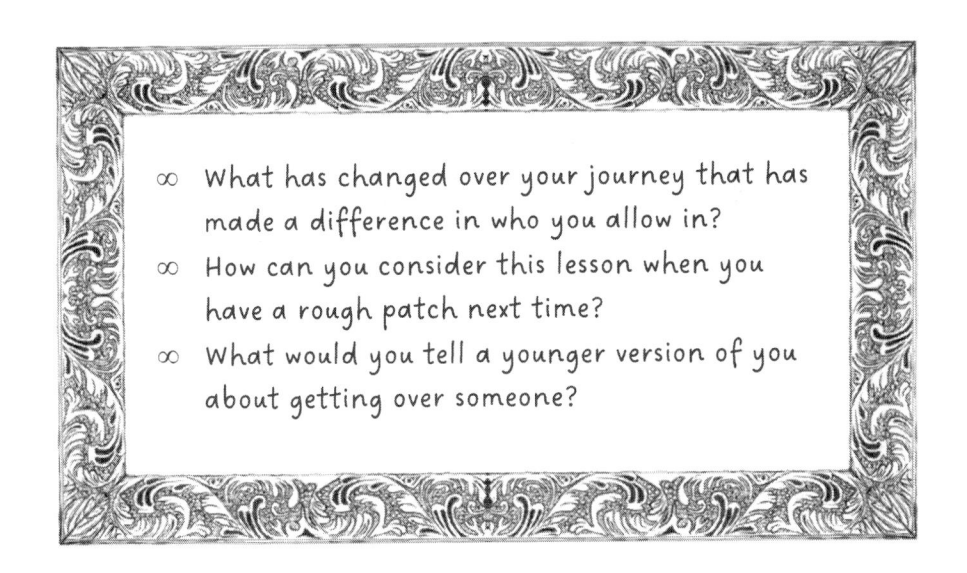

- ∞ What has changed over your journey that has made a difference in who you allow in?
- ∞ How can you consider this lesson when you have a rough patch next time?
- ∞ What would you tell a younger version of you about getting over someone?

Some days you have to take a step forward in your journey leaving someone behind who you love very much.

The reason doesn't matter.

Sometimes it is as simple as having busy lives or relocating. But it could be bigger like changing values, or even death.

That doesn't change what you have to deal with today. What matters is that you still take a step forward in your journey.

Some steps might be taken with a tear in your eye as you miss your person not being by your side.

Some days you might glance over to share a laugh or smile and feel your heart sink just a little when you realize they are not there.

But you step forward anyway.

Some steps might be taken in spite, to show them you can still make it without them.

Some might be taken in fear, not knowing if you can clear the obstacles in your way without having a guide through the messes life throws at you.

But you step forward anyway.

You are who you are as a result of everyone you have encountered up until this point in time. Even if they are no longer in your life. They have all played a part, whether it felt good or not so great. They moved you forward to be who you are today.

The days you celebrate are their celebration too, though perhaps they are in another place.

So, when you take that step, when it doesn't feel great to do it alone, stop to reflect on those who you wish were still by your side.

Stop to think about those you are glad are no longer holding you back.

Take a moment to honor those who are not here and know that they are still part of your journey today.

Step forward knowing everyone you have loved has loved you because of the part of your journey they were blessed to be a part of.

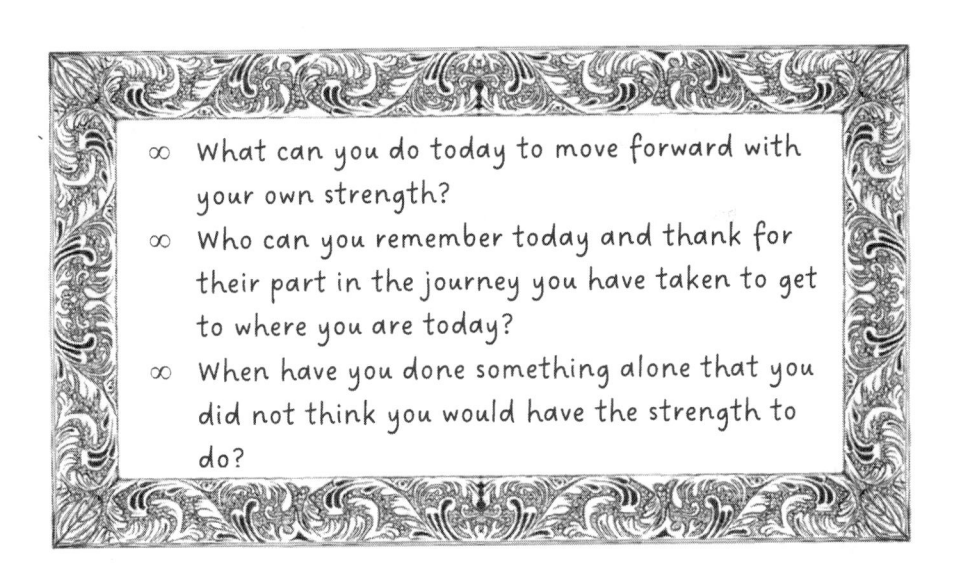

- ∞ What can you do today to move forward with your own strength?
- ∞ Who can you remember today and thank for their part in the journey you have taken to get to where you are today?
- ∞ When have you done something alone that you did not think you would have the strength to do?

Sometimes you get good news.

Sometimes you get bad news.

Sometimes you get no news at all.

The good-news days feel amazing. You feel confident, excited for life, content.

You can't wait to see what comes next.

The bad-news days are rough. You do what you can to get through, but its not easy.

Adrenaline and instinct seem to be the only things to get you from one minute to the next.

The no-news days are tricky.

There isn't a reason to be down, but after the high of good news, or the emotions surrounding bad news, it's hard not to interpret the nothingness as something bad.

You forget that every day can't be a good-news day.

But there is a reason for the nothing days. They serve a purpose almost greater than any.

The nothing days are what reset your emotions. They balance your expectations.

They allow you to feel.

For without a nothing day, you would never feel the highs of the good-news days.
For without the nothing days, you would never be prepared emotionally to face the bad-news days.

Nothing days recalibrate your soul while they reset your ability to both cope with the bad and enjoy the good.

Live your life my friends, making the most of every good-news day you can, while making it through the bad-news days.

All the while, using the nothing days as a guide to come back to as you experience the ebb and flow of life.

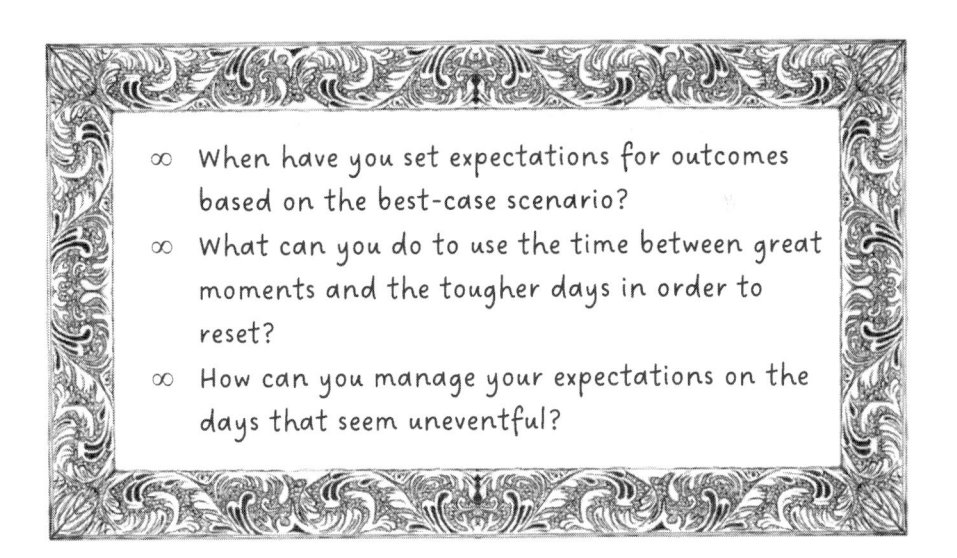

- ∞ When have you set expectations for outcomes based on the best-case scenario?
- ∞ What can you do to use the time between great moments and the tougher days in order to reset?
- ∞ How can you manage your expectations on the days that seem uneventful?

Sometimes you have people surrounding you who tell you all of the reasons you will not succeed.

They seem to be there every step of your journey, looking, waiting, hoping to see you trip.

Then, as if you didn't feel the pain of your own stumble, they point out the fall. They tell you what you did wrong as if you should have seen it coming ahead of time.

They seem only to delight in your setbacks. Yet they are never there to celebrate your wins.

These are not your people.

They pretend to be.

But they are not.

They may say they have your best interest at heart. That they are only here to help.

In fact, they are afraid to take the risks to succeed in their own lives and feel the only power they have comes from finding flaws in yours.

Your stumbles are yours to learn from.

Your failures are yours to own.

Their insecurities and fears of trying are not for you to answer to.

Stay on your path my friends. Know that there will be false allies along the way.
When they try to bring you down, don't let them succeed.

Simply take another step forward and leave them behind.

Just keep moving forward. Keep stumbling.

Continue to fail.

But don't listen to those who are sitting on the sidelines afraid to play the game.

Take another step towards your future and never look back to see them trying to slow you down.

Your journey is yours. You are on your way to your best life.

And your best life is created through the lessons you learn with every stumble you make along the way.

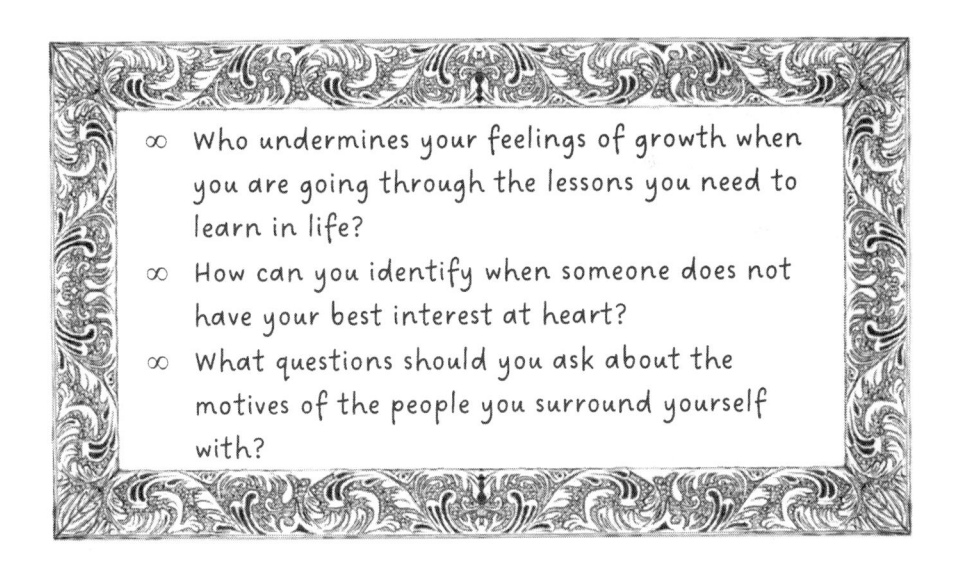

- ∞ Who undermines your feelings of growth when you are going through the lessons you need to learn in life?
- ∞ How can you identify when someone does not have your best interest at heart?
- ∞ What questions should you ask about the motives of the people you surround yourself with?

Sometimes you see someone from before.

Before you changed, before you found peace, before you found your passion.

You aren't even sure if you recognize them at first, but there's a familiar smile in their eyes that you can't get past.

You make the connection. You reconnect.

They ask what you've been up to and how things have been.

Yet you just don't even know where to start.

You try to fill them in, but you've come so far it seems like there is so much you forget to mention.

You knew them before the wheel was invented and now you're soaring among the stars.

How do you explain the evolution of travel from carts, to race-cars, to flight, and now space travel?

You don't.

They are meeting you were you are now.

They can see you are no longer on that dusty dirt road traveling alone at a snails-pace.

They see you soaring and man are they happy to meet you here above the clouds.

They can tell you have come so far and they don't really care how. They are just happy you've made it here.

So you connect.

You recollect the good times you shared.

You recall the challenges you're happy you've both moved past.

And you start a new page in your story in a fresh setting together.

In that moment you can look at where you have come, what you've done, and you finally understand how much life has changed since you decided to take control of your destiny.

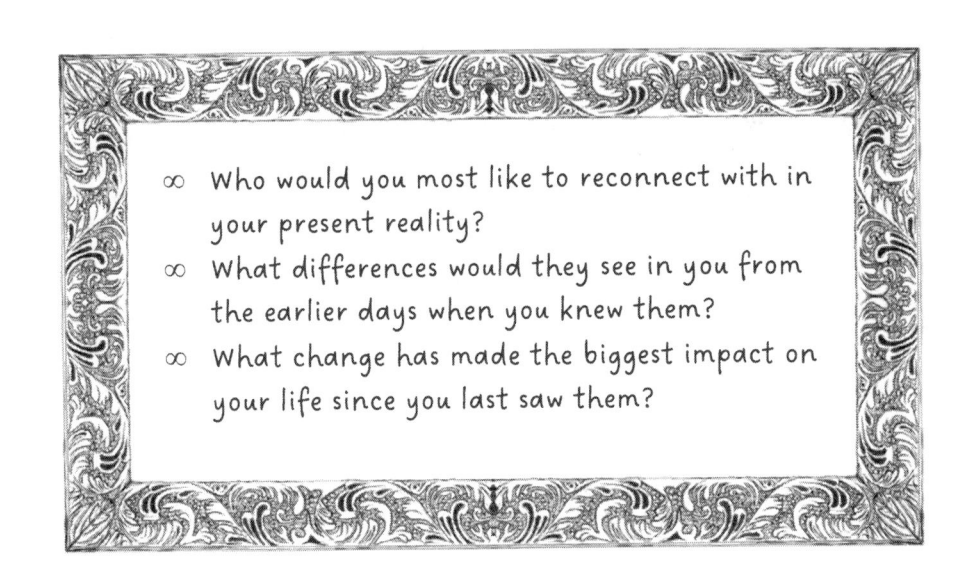

- ∞ Who would you most like to reconnect with in your present reality?
- ∞ What differences would they see in you from the earlier days when you knew them?
- ∞ What change has made the biggest impact on your life since you last saw them?

Sometimes you are stuck living in a memory you want so desperately to forget.

A moment in time that seems to live on for eternity in the recesses of your mind.

It's not always calling you, but when you close your eyes and relax, it seeps through the cracks in your thoughts and takes over.

Before you even notice, it's the main feature on the screen inside your head.

You can't look away. Feelings have already settled in and without warning you are back in that place, reliving the moment like you've never left. Never moved on.

It feels just like you're there.

The hurt.

The fear.

The pain.

But that's just how your brain works. It doesn't know that this is just a memory.

It's forgotten for a moment that you have moved on.

It's tricked by the images in your head to make you feel like you're still that person lost in the world.

But you're not lost. And you have moved on.

And the beauty in this dark moment is that it is just an illusion.

It is just a memory.

You can open your eyes and live again in a new world.

Even though the memory will come back, it will always be just that, an unwelcome visitor that won't stay for long.

Life isn't the absence of struggles my friend. It's what we do to overcome them and what we celebrate between the tough times that makes it worth living.

Open your eyes, leave the nightmares in the dark and carry on my friend.

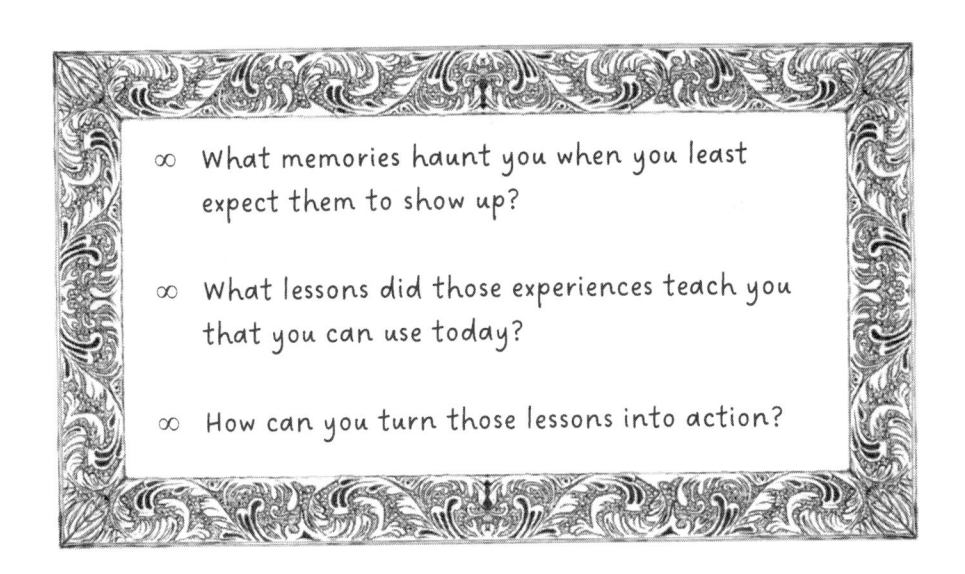

∞ What memories haunt you when you least expect them to show up?

∞ What lessons did those experiences teach you that you can use today?

∞ How can you turn those lessons into action?

What is the real issue here?

Imagine continually bailing buckets of water out of a flooded boat but never bothering to find the leak and plug the hole.

All too often we treat the symptoms while ignoring the disease. The symptoms are easier to treat. When you relieve the pain, they go away at least for a moment.

But if the cause is not identified, the same symptoms will only return as soon as the drugs wear off, the boat will fill up again with water. You will not have solved the problem, only set it aside to be dealt with another day.

Find the real issue in your life right now. Look past the distractions and identify what really needs to be solved in order to live the life you want.

Sometimes you drive down a dark highway in the depth of night.

Towards the world you want, or away from one you can't handle, you can't be sure. But you drive on anyway.

The journey calms your senses until you are numb to the outside world.

You feel in control, heading somewhere. Even though you are going nowhere in particular.

The road lulls your thoughts to sleep as the monotony of the drive takes over your consciousness.

You can't see the destination, but you're sure it will bring you happiness.

You know it will solve your problems.

You are confident that when you arrive, your troubles will be over.

So you continue to drive on.

To somewhere. To anywhere. To nowhere.

You don't stop.

The spell the road has cast upon you is strong. The safety in the ubiquitous journey protects your mind and shields your heart.

But you will never arrive.
As soon as you stop driving the lull of the road settles, and you hear life again.

But this time you hear more than just the troubles.

You hear laughter, music, and friendly voices.

You hear the things you were driving away from that you didn't know you left behind.

Now they carry a melody sweeter than you ever heard.

Slow your drive my friend. For the scary things you face can overpower the sounds of all the good you are surrounded by.

Let the good voices be heard, the beautiful song be sung, and the laughter be enjoyed.

Life is a journey enjoyed best when you listen to all of the life around you.

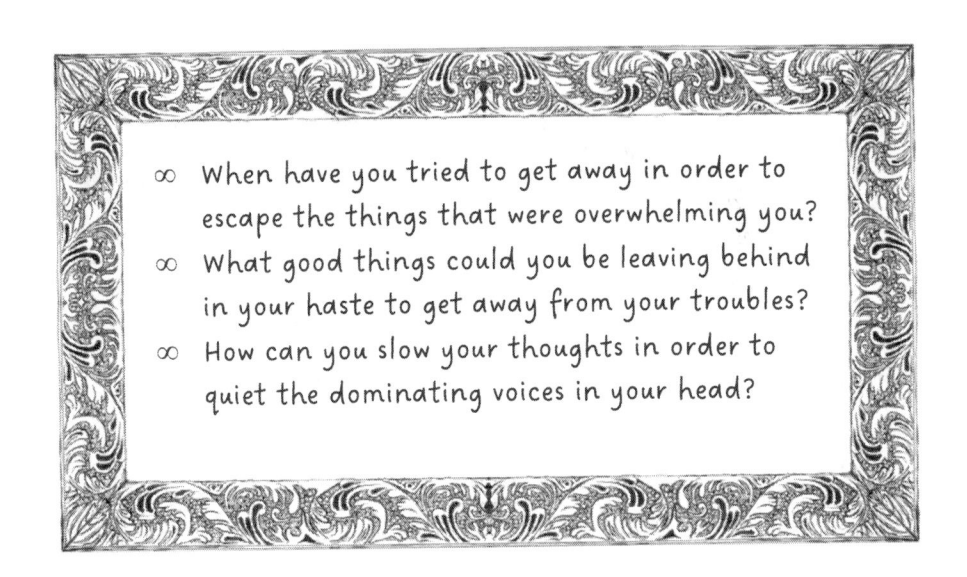

∞ When have you tried to get away in order to escape the things that were overwhelming you?
∞ What good things could you be leaving behind in your haste to get away from your troubles?
∞ How can you slow your thoughts in order to quiet the dominating voices in your head?

Sometimes you get attention, and it feels good. But it doesn't quite feel right.

You're glad to be noticed.

You're flattered to receive the compliments.

Yet you grapple with the thought that something isn't complete.

It could be you. It could be them. It could just be the mood in the air tonight.

Regardless, you take the words for what they are and nothing more.

Maybe they paid you compliments with an ulterior motive. Maybe not.

Maybe they have feelings for you which you are not ready to return.

You consider it.

You'd like to explore feelings with someone. But they aren't the one.

A part of them seems like they could be the one. You could talk yourself into thinking the rest of them is.

But that's what got you into the wrong situations in the past. Situations you'd like to say you've learned from.

Have you?

They are here, but that is just an opportunity of chance.

And you're both worth so much more.

Or perhaps you misread the mood entirely.

It doesn't really matter either way.

Enjoy the evening. Partake in the company. But keep the boundaries where they need to be.

And when you turn them down, do it with kindness and respect.

For on other nights you could be on the other side of this equation and that doesn't always feel so good.

But if you do it right you can at least say when it was your turn to say no, you were able to treat people well and walk away in kindness.

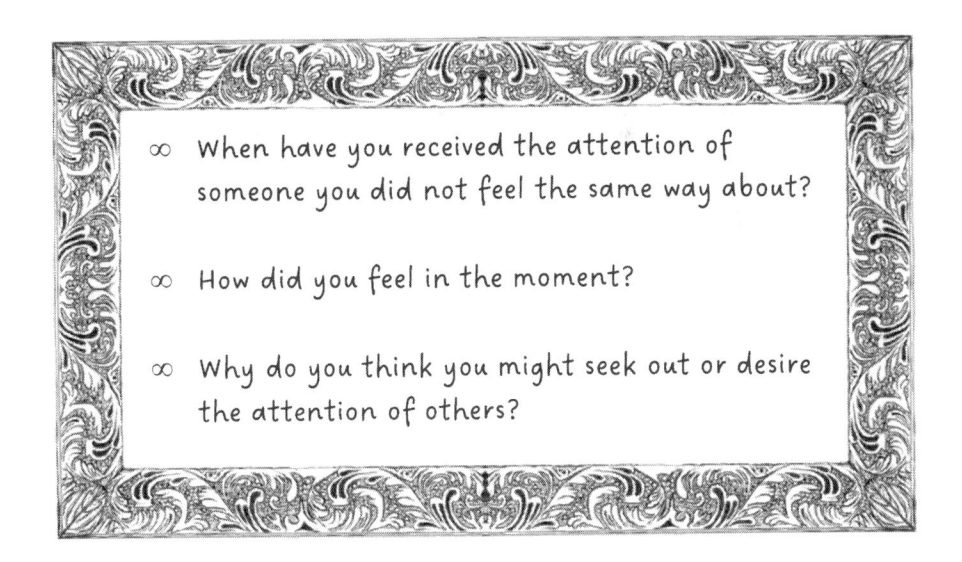

- ∞ When have you received the attention of someone you did not feel the same way about?

- ∞ How did you feel in the moment?

- ∞ Why do you think you might seek out or desire the attention of others?

Sometimes you walk away.

You put your drink down and you leave the party.

You don't make a scene. You don't throw a fit. You simply say your goodbyes and move along.

Nothing bad happened. No one hurt you. No one made you feel unwelcome. You just know it's time to go.

You've had your fun and can see where the night is going. And that's not a place you care to go.

You exit.

You walk away knowing you made the right choice for you.

That's all that matters.

Your friends asked you to stay. They even offered to buy your next round.

But it's not about them. It's about you.

You have bigger plans. Your plans need you to be fresh tomorrow. To be level-headed as you end tonight.

Sure, you can have your fun when the time comes. But tonight your dreams beckon.

You walk home with the sounds of music and laughter fading in the distance.

You don't feel like you're missing out. Rather you're just walking towards something different.

Something bigger.

Something just for you.

The life you desire.

That's how it goes my friends. You can't always stay at the party when you have a ball to attend later.

You have to walk away knowing better things are in store for you.

And it doesn't have to be a bad thing at all.

Leave the party. Let them chase you with the glass slipper.

And all the while, make that fairytale come true for yourself.

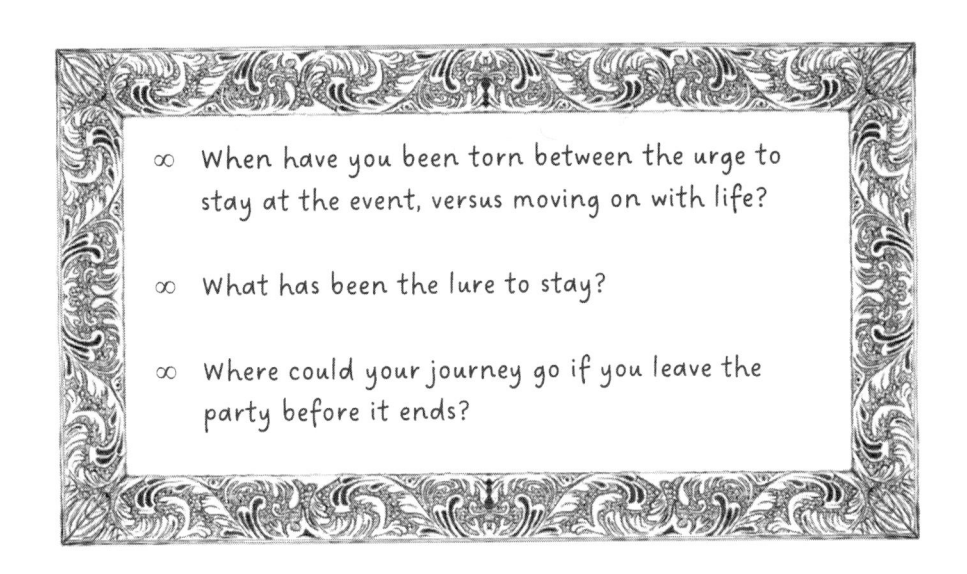

- ∞ When have you been torn between the urge to stay at the event, versus moving on with life?
- ∞ What has been the lure to stay?
- ∞ Where could your journey go if you leave the party before it ends?

Sometimes you attract the wrong person.

You give off the vibe and you don't even know it. They're hooked, but you're not reeling in the line.

You're just being you. Doing your thing.

They find it attractive.

They move towards you. They make their intentions known.

To be honest it isn't all that bad. After all, you've been looking for someone to want you this whole time.

You've longed for the day when someone looks your direction with the desire they have in their eyes.

Yet it doesn't move you like it did when the dream played out in your mind.

In fact you want to run away. You want to cut the line.

It messes with your head.

Are you expecting too much?

Should you turn down this attention you've wanted for so long?

Yes. You absolutely should.

You need to close the doors that aren't right for you to enter.

You need to pass on the chances that are easy just because they are right in front of you.

For if you enter that room you leave behind the chance to meet the one that really is right for you.

They'll walk down the hallway and see you're busy in another room.

They'll see you're taken.

And they won't give you a second thought.

Stay free. Stay available. And know that you will one day attract the right one.

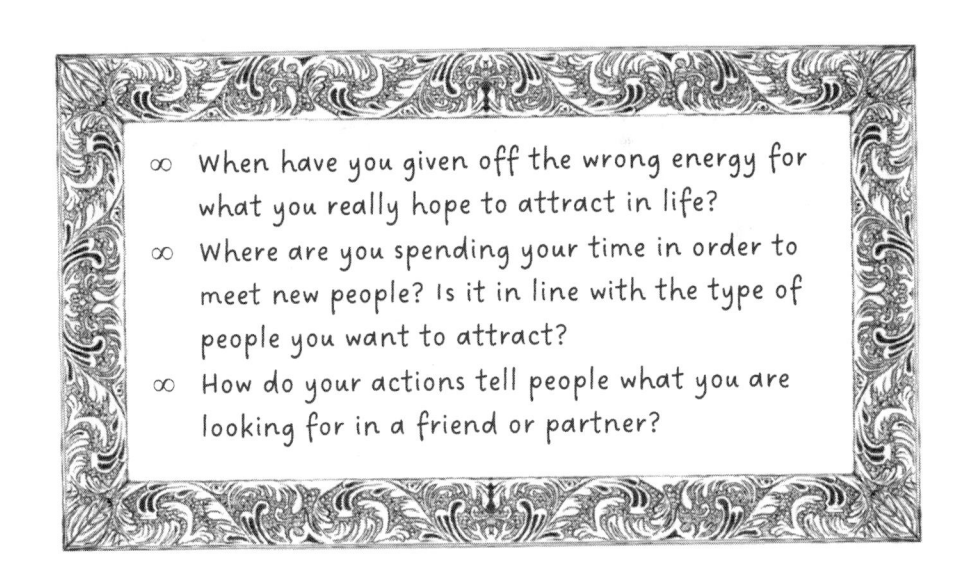

- ∞ When have you given off the wrong energy for what you really hope to attract in life?
- ∞ Where are you spending your time in order to meet new people? Is it in line with the type of people you want to attract?
- ∞ How do your actions tell people what you are looking for in a friend or partner?

Sometimes you sit in the aftermath of your own bad decisions amidst a silence so loud its beat hurts your eardrums.

You look around at the rubble surrounding you.

It seems you can't take a single step in any direction without first clearing some sort of debris out of your way.

You're angry. You're lost. You're overwhelmed.

You blame anything and anyone but yourself for the mess you're in.

It feels better to point a finger than to lift a hand to start the clean-up effort.

But the blame doesn't matter. Nothing changes.

Whether you have the right to assign it to another, or owe it all to yourself, it doesn't change what needs to be done.

So you sit. You look around.

You wonder, where should you even try to start.

All you can see is the mess. But somewhere underneath it all, is solid ground.

You can't see it now, but you will find it some day. And on this foundation you will rebuild.

Finally, you accept that only you can take the action to clear the mess.

You begin to move the things closest to you out of the way.

Maybe you make a path out of where you are so you can get some help to lift the biggest pieces.

You prepare your world to be rebuilt.

Things start to look better as the silence quiets itself to a dull roar.

You begin to hear life again.

You start to feel hope.

You can see a way out. Because you did something to make it better.

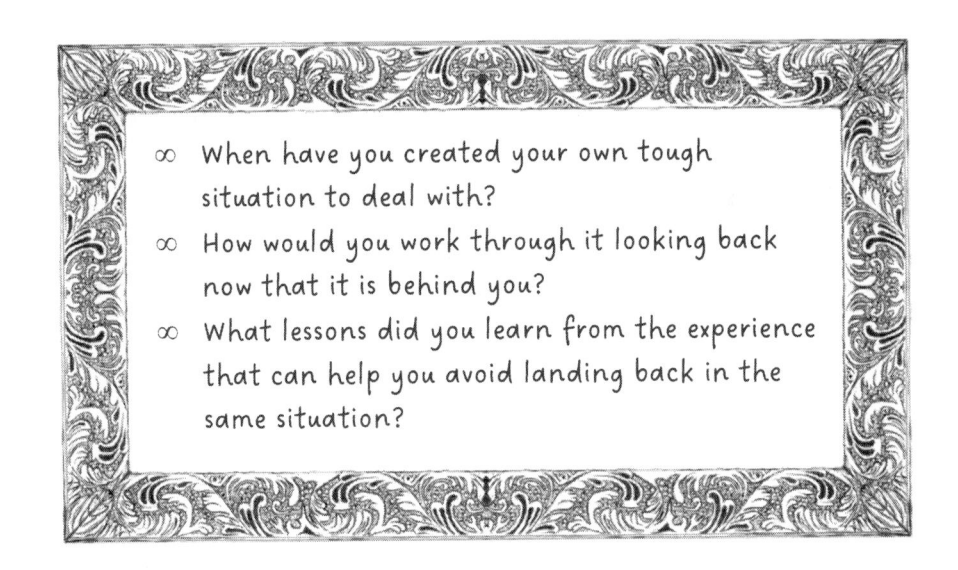

> - ∞ When have you created your own tough situation to deal with?
> - ∞ How would you work through it looking back now that it is behind you?
> - ∞ What lessons did you learn from the experience that can help you avoid landing back in the same situation?

Sometimes you roam the city streets in the darkest hour.

The shadows hide the imperfections while also protecting you from the hazards of the unknown.

You take another step forward because you have no choice but to keep moving.

To stop is to give in to your fears. Or is it?

Is it braver to march on so that your footsteps disguise the noises you can't explain than it is to pause and listen to the unknown?

Is the fear of knowing the only thing that keeps you racing ever forward?

Step by step you move through the night towards a day that teases you with the illusion of safety. A day that promises security and light.

But the light will only expose the things the night hides.

They are still there. They have always been there.

Only in the day, you cannot pretend they don't exist.

You muster the courage to stop. To still the motion.

To wait for the sound of fear to penetrate your ears.

At first there is nothing. Just the beating of your heart in concert with the rhythm of your breath.

But then the symphony of your body gives way to the noises of the night.

They are the noises you can't explain. The sounds that you feel before you hear.

They are the world you've tried to avoid which you thought the night would hide.

But it's still there, behind the shadows. Always with you.

Suddenly you understand, the challenges and fears you face remain within reach even when they are out of sight.

Day or night, they must be faced, but you can do it.

Each challenge, every fear, you face gets you one step closer my friend to being able to Own Your Awkward.

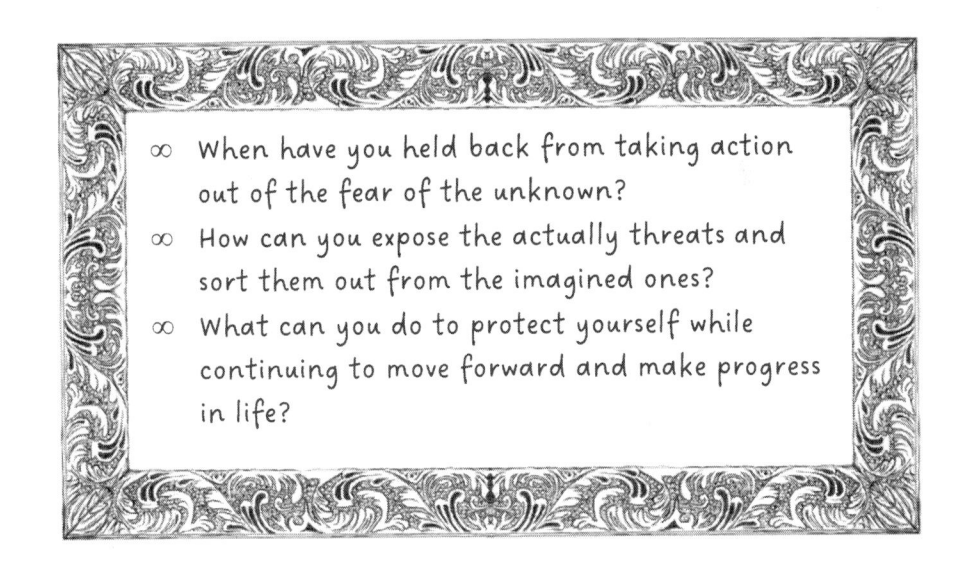

- ∞ When have you held back from taking action out of the fear of the unknown?
- ∞ How can you expose the actually threats and sort them out from the imagined ones?
- ∞ What can you do to protect yourself while continuing to move forward and make progress in life?

Sometimes you get absolutely dumped on. We all know the saying, when it rains it pours.

Today it's pouring buckets.

You try to dodge the raindrops, but there seems to be no place to stand which isn't affected.

You feel your skin getting wet. Your vision getting blurry as the water runs down your face and clouds your eyes.

You wonder how much water has dumped on you. There's no way you can quantify it no matter how hard you try.

All the while the rain falls. And the downpour continues.

By now it's a distraction. Calling your attention to the trials dumped on you and pulling your focus away from what you can do about it.

What can you do?

You can take stock of every drop that hits you blow by blow. You can argue how unfair it is and find evidence as to why you don't deserve this.

All the while the water level rises around you.

You could drown in this rising tide of setbacks.

If you stay focused on the downpour the storm wins.

So why not take another course.

Buy an umbrella to keep your head dry. Learn to swim, or at least to tread water.

Find a life raft to pull yourself up out of the water into.

You can practice any skill that will move you one step out of this mess.

It isn't easy when the blows are still coming. But it is not impossible.

Take a moment right now to look away from the downpour. Find the driest patch you can.

And do one thing no matter how small to take control of the circumstances you find yourself in today.

You got this my friend. We will always have a rainy season come and go in our lives.

But sunnier days are yet to come.

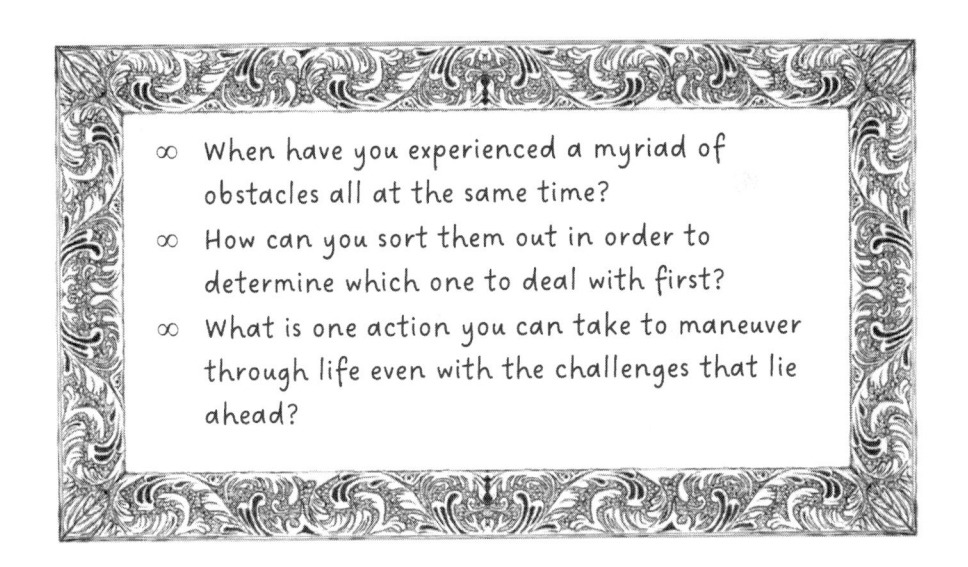

- ∞ When have you experienced a myriad of obstacles all at the same time?
- ∞ How can you sort them out in order to determine which one to deal with first?
- ∞ What is one action you can take to maneuver through life even with the challenges that lie ahead?

Sometimes you sit in a boat that has just been rocked.

Something, or perhaps more likely, someone disturbed it.

But it doesn't really matter what the cause was.

Either way, you are left in the wake of its actions.

Tossing side to side.

Suspended above a sea of insecurities you cannot see. Though you sense they are there waiting for you to be tossed overboard.

The boat rocks to one side so you lean to the other. Using all of your weight to counter the direction the boat is trying to toss you.

Perhaps you've overcompensated as it now feels inevitable that it will through you out the other side.

The more you fight the worse it gets.

It seems inevitable that this will not end well.

It's scary when your boat is rocked.

You feel like you have no control. And the more you try to get it, the less you have.

But this is life my friends.

The key to getting control is letting go of the urge to try to capture it.
Once you stop trying.

Once you relax.

The boat will settle.

Hunker down.

Relax.

Take a deep breath.

Let the boat move as it will.

For it's taking your lead. And this my friends is the start to a more peaceful life.

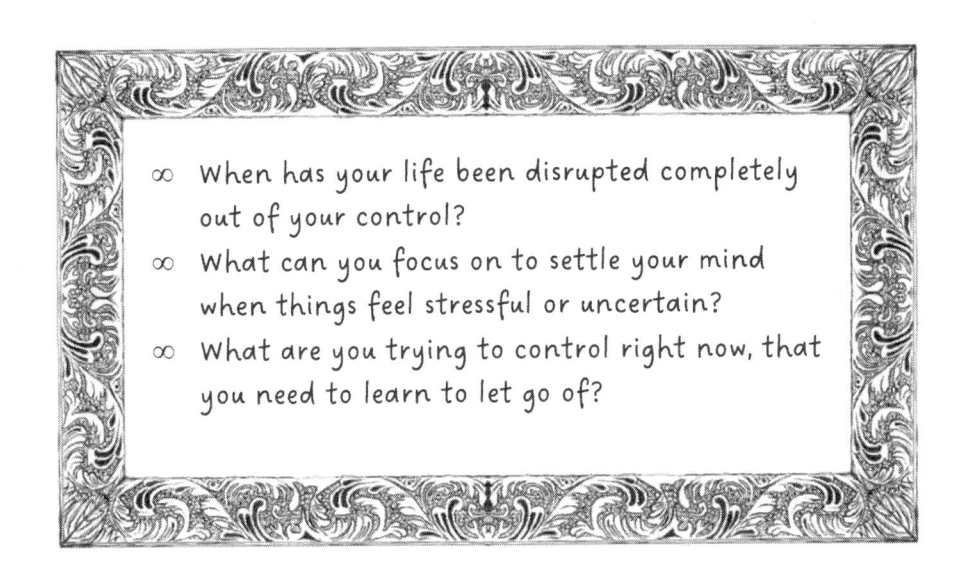

- ∞ When has your life been disrupted completely out of your control?
- ∞ What can you focus on to settle your mind when things feel stressful or uncertain?
- ∞ What are you trying to control right now, that you need to learn to let go of?

Sometimes you get to the end. You make it to your goal.

You finish.

All that is left to do now is wait for the feelings of accomplishment to flood in. They may or they may not.

They might come for a moment but only stay like the fleeting light from a bolt of lightning. Leaving you with questions of what to do next.

Which way should you turn?

The success is yours to keep. You made it. You finished. You accomplished what you set out to do.

Even though the feeling of success will subside, the fact that you completed your project will always be a badge you can wear with honor.

But how do you get the feeling back?

How do you stay in that moment of accomplishment.

Well, you cannot stay there for long in reality. But you can recreate it.

You can start a journey down a new path, towards a different adventure.

You can go back to the beginning and relive the moments of self-discovery you have already experienced on this part of your journey, looking for ways to take your experience to an even deeper level.

It is a cruel trick of our minds that the feeling of success comes during the process of doing the work to be successful more so than in the final achievement.

Reflect back on what it tool for you to accomplish this last goal. Think about how it felt on the days you were truly productive. That is where you will find the feeling again.

Find a new project, a new goal. Start the next part of your journey. Along the way, you will recreate the feeling you just felt.

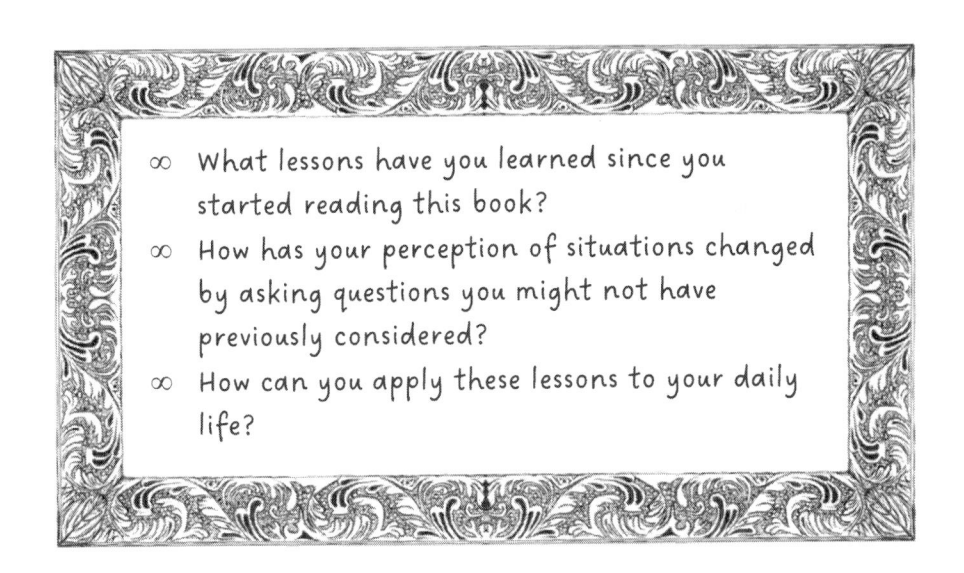

- ∞ What lessons have you learned since you started reading this book?
- ∞ How has your perception of situations changed by asking questions you might not have previously considered?
- ∞ How can you apply these lessons to your daily life?

So you made it through the whole book. You've spent sixty days reflecting on the way you think in any given situation. You have read the thoughts that rave through my mind and have questioned similar situations you have experienced in your own life.

So now you may wonder what comes next. Have you reframed your mind in a way that you will never again be bothered with a lonely thought? Will you no longer struggle through a painful moment?

The short answer is, no. There is no magic cure that will take you away from ever experiencing a challenging moment in your life. That is just reality.

It is the tough moments that act as anchor for the highs we experience. We cannot appreciate the good times if we do not have the contrast of the daily challenges.

So, what do you have?

You have tools. You have experience. You have a new perspective.

You see, reframing is not something that happens once. It is not a set-it-and-forget-it cure to life. Reframing is an act you will need to constantly do each time you encounter a less than ideal set of circumstances.

But you are now armed with tools to approach these with a new light. You have practiced these tools over the last two months, and you will continue to strengthen your reframing muscles with each challenge you encounter.

My last thought to leave with you is to not step too far away from the mindset you are in right now. Don't set this book down and walk away without looking back.

Keep the key reframing questions on the next page close to you. Refer back to them as often as needed. Write them down and put them in your pocket so they are always with you.

Practice every day to reframe at least one situation you are facing, big or small. By continually working these muscles you will get better and better and mastering your own frame of mind.

By reframing even the smallest of challenges, you strengthen your skills as a master reframe. Preparing you to face the biggest and toughest situations which still lie ahead.

You can do it. I know it is in you. It all starts with changing the way you are looking at the road ahead.

Key Questions to Reframe Your Thoughts

- ∞ What is the best possible outcome of this situation?

- ∞ What would you tell someone else if they were going through the same thing?

- ∞ When have you felt like this in the past and made it through just fine?

- ∞ What other factors could be at play affecting how you feel right now?

- ∞ How can you tell this story in a different way with a better ending?

- ∞ What is the real issue here?

More Books by Andy Vargo

Own Your Awkward Life Changes is the complete handbook for mastering the changes you will continues to face for the rest of your life.

Choose the sixty-day guided journal that is right for the net part of your journey.

For discounts on bulk quantities for your book club or organization please contact andy@awkwardcareer.com

About the Author

Andy Vargo is no stranger to change!

If you ever feel awkward about yourself, then you can understand how Andy Vargo lived the first forty years of his life. Coming out of the closet at forty doesn't define him, pursuing his passion to help others does. Having changed everything about his life, Andy leads others as a motivational speaker and helps people live their fullest lives as a life coach. At night you can find him working stages around the northwest as a comedian making light of his journey with the gift of laughter.

Awkward is not only his brand, but his style as Andy encourages us all to 'Own Your Awkward' and be true to your genuine self.

Andy hosts the podcast, *Own Your Awkward*, authored Own Your Awkward Life Changes, The Awkward Journal series, and shares his thoughts and ideas in his blog and video series available at awkwardcareer.com.

Made in the USA
Middletown, DE
29 July 2025